THE FIRST DETECTIVE

The Police of New York City

robert l. bryan

Published by robert l. bryan, 2023.

THE FIRST DETECTIVE

First edition. July 27, 2023.

Copyright © 2023 robert l. bryan.

ISBN: 979-8223353249

Written by robert l. bryan.

For Meghan, the angel on my shoulder.

Introduction:

In the second half of the 19th century, women in New York City faced a range of challenges and limitations in their daily lives. Many were expected to conform to strict gender roles and were excluded from many areas of public life, including politics and higher education. Family life was central to their existence. Women were expected to marry and have children, and their primary role was to manage the household and care for their families. Women who were unmarried or childless were often viewed with suspicion and were seen as somehow deficient or incomplete. Marriage was therefore highly valued, and women were expected to prioritize finding a suitable husband.

Once married, a women's life revolved around her husband and children. She was responsible for maintaining a clean and orderly home, cooking, and cleaning, and caring for the children. Women had few opportunities for leisure activities or hobbies, as their time was consumed by domestic duties. They also had little control over their own lives, as their husbands had legal and social authority over them.

While some women worked outside the home, this was relatively uncommon. Those who did work were largely confined to a few occupations, such as domestic service, factory work, or teaching. Women in these fields often faced low wages and poor working conditions and were subjected to discrimination and harassment on the job.

The New York City Police Department was born in 1845 but at that time policework was off limits to women. It would take many years for women to establish their story in the NYPD. That story is both impressive and heroic, but it is also a story that is still in progress, where there is more to be written and achieved. Having strong, skilled members and leaders of the NYPD, both women and men, who know their communities and the pressures of everyday life, is critical to protecting the city. The unique perspectives and experiences of women are essential to achieving that goal.

The story of the NYPD is a story that was exclusively male until women were introduced into the department as matrons. By 1918, six policewomen had been appointed to the uniformed force, and the next year, the first African American woman joined the NYPD. By 1934, women were allowed to have pistol practice with the male officers.

In 1961 the Police Commissioner did not believe women had the physical strength or the endurance to be sergeants, so Gertrude Schimmel and Felicia Shpritzer sued for the right of women to take promotional exams—a case they eventually won. In 1965 Shpritzer and Schimmel became the first women sergeants. Shpritzer retired as a lieutenant while Gertrude "Gertie" Schimmel would go on to be named the first female chief of the NYPD in 1978—more than 130 years after the founding of the Department. It is hard for us to imagine how difficult it must have been for those early women to rise in the ranks of the NYPD, when we know that the challenges continue today after nearly a century's worth of work. Today, women make up almost 35 percent of the NYPD and 17 percent of the uniformed force.

Just as we recognize the trailblazers, it is important that we remember the stories of those whose time as part of the thin blue line was cut all too short. The first woman of the NYPD killed in the line of duty was Irma, or Fran, Lozada. I shared a classroom with Fran when we both attended the police academy in 1981. She was a plainclothes transit officer and had been pursuing a suspect who had snatched a gold chain from an unsuspecting victim on the L train. She followed him to a nearby warehouse yard where the suspect wrestled her gun from her and shot her.

I was one of more than 3,500 police officers who lined the streets to say goodbye to Officer Lozada on a dreary day in September 1984. The crowd's grief was echoed by the haunting tones of the Emerald Society's Pipes & Drums, which always simultaneously evoke deeply felt emotions of mourning, respect, and the celebration of a brave life.

The stories of women like Irma Lozada, and Gertrude Schimmel are the stories of New York and the NYPD—both uplifting and heartbreaking. These women were all gritty and courageous, dedicated and humble, selfless and stalwart. Their qualities are the qualities that define the NYPD.

The famous author Rudyard Kipling said: "If history were taught in the form of stories, it would never be forgotten." [1] In honor of Mr. Kipling's quote, I present a brief story.

The customer listened intently as Vesta, the 50-year-old fortuneteller described a soul kiss. "You gaze into the eyes of your affinity and your soul leaps into his eyes and into his soul. That's the soul kiss. There is no smack to it, and it's not at all like other kisses. But after the soul kiss has taken place there is perfect harmony between the souls and there couldn't be any misunderstanding. It is a guarantee of a happy marriage – five dollars please." Vesta saw the powerful force created by the soul kiss and gave up her life to teach others how to soul kiss in the proper fashion – at a reasonable rate.

The plainly clothed, neat looking woman who had breezed into her Manhattan parlor of occultism was not interested in a soul kiss. She wanted her palm read. Vesta shook her head. "Reading palms is nix," said the prophetess. Close both your eyes."

The customer obediently closed both eyes.

"Now look into my face with your third eye, which is situated accurately in the middle of your forehead. Look hard! Now what do you see?"

"I see green," said the customer as she opened her eyes to make sure the madame was not extracting green from her pocketbook.

Vesta looked at the customer sadly. "Ah!" she said, "then your soul is green – five dollars please, but wait, you have not wished. Breathe a wish!"

"How do you breathe a wish?" asked the customer.

"You just breathe it," explained the madame.

"Alright, I breathe a wish to get married," said the customer.

"You will be married in five days – five dollars please."

"But how will I know the man?" asked the customer."

"Whenever you see a man in whom you are interested, soul kiss him."

The customer cringed. "But I can't go around soul kissing men like that – I'd be arrested."

Vesta shook her head. "You did not understand what I said before," and she repeated her definition of the soul kiss. "And the charge is five dollars," she finished up.

The customer slightly smiled and displayed a police shield. "The charge is disorderly conduct," declared Detective Sergeant Isabella Goodwin. [2]

In this book I share the complete story of a pioneer in the NYPD, who was instrumental in shaping where women have been in the department and where they are going. This is the story of Isabella Goodwin – the first detective.

Chapter 1: A Cop's Wife

Isabella Loghry was born in Greenwich Village, Manhattan in 1865 to James Harvey Loghry and Anna J. Monteith, who ran a restaurant and hotel on Canal Street. When she was young, Isabella aspired to be an opera singer, but in 1885, at the age of 19, she married John W. Goodwin, a police officer, and assumed the traditional role of a woman taking care of the home and family. They had two children in the early days of their life together, but Isabella had already discovered, like the criminals she would one day try to bring to justice, that life could deal out unfathomable challenges.

John Goodwin became a member of the New York Police Department on August 29, 1882, and due to the experience she had gained from her parent's restaurant, Isabella and her husband operated a restaurant at the landmark Willow Cottage, on Eleventh Avenue between Twenty-second and Twenty-third Streets, to stretch the family income.

John's police career did not get off to a good start. During the remaining months of 1882 Goodwin was brought up on departmental charges numerous times.

9/12/82 – fined 3 days for being absent from post in a liquor store and on the same day fined one day for losing his shield.

10/10/82 – fined one day for improper patrol, and an additional three days on the same day for improper patrol.

11/1/82 – fined 2 days and 5 days for improper patrol and sleeping on post.

11/22/82 – fined five days for being absent from post in a liquor store, and an additional two days for being found in the hallway of a liquor store, and two days for being absent from roll call.

11/28/82 – fined thirty days for being found in the condition of delirium tremens – a condition of severe alcohol withdrawal with symptoms such as shaking, confusion and hallucinations.

Goodwin was able to keep his job and get his act together well enough to avoid any further charges and to obtain a promotion to roundsman in 1884. A roundsman was a rank between a patrolman and sergeant which was abolished in the early part of the twentieth century. Many of John's problems were alcohol-related, but he seemed to be able to control the problem. He was working in the Fourth Precinct and was supporting his family right up until the summer of 1889.

...

William Griffin had been trying to squeeze out a living selling sewing machines for the Singer Company for four months. On July 17th, 1889, he tried a new building within his assigned area. Mary Ryners answered the doorbell of her first-floor apartment at 229 East 105th Street and sighed in disgust when she saw she was facing a salesman. Despite his animated sales pitch, Mrs. Ryners shook her head and closed her apartment door.

Like any good salesman, Griffin was not going to miss an opportunity. He was already in the building, and he planned on taking advantage of his situation. He lugged his sales kit up the stairs and knocked on the door on the second-floor landing. John Goodwin came to the door and after only a few seconds of his sales pitch, Goodwin growled, "No!"

Griffin began down the stairs as Goodwin called out asking what authority Griffin had to be in the building. Griffin handed Goodwin a brochure for the sewing machine, but Goodwin scoffed at the document and said anyone could get it. Goodwin wanted to know how Griffin had gotten inside the building and Griffin said Mrs. Ryners had let him in. Goodwin escorted Griffin downstairs where Mary Ryners first denied letting Griffin in, but then admitted she had allowed him entry. Goodwin told Griffin to get out, but when he turned to leave the building Goodwin struck him from behind, knocking him down. Goodwin proceeded to drag Griffin outside where he placed him under arrest at 3rd Avenue and 105th Street. Once at the station house the officer in command verified Griffin's identity and released him. Goodwin was charged with striking a civilian.

...

William Smith was a Doorman assigned to the Fourth Precinct in 1888. The precinct doorman, an official NYPD rank below that of Patrolman was a combination turnkey/custodian – he was responsible for the upkeep of the stationhouse, guarding and sometimes transporting prisoners, shoveling coal and taking out the ashes. They would also make sure the men were awake after reserve duty. On August 8, 1889, Smith went on duty at 6 P.M. and worked until 8 A.M. on the 9th.

John Goodwin was the acting sergeant working the desk. At 12:20 A.M. he dismissed the men going home and those dismissed for reserve went to bed. During that era policemen worked long hours with mandatory patrol and reserve time. When a patrolman finished his shift, he did not necessarily go home. He could be starting his mandatory reserve time where he would go to the designated area in the station house to sleep, being subject to be activated for patrol in case of an emergency.

A short time after the incoming officers had been dismissed for home and reserve, officers from the Society for the Prevention of Cruelty to Children brought two prisoners into the station house. As the desk officer, Goodwin properly entered their information in the blotter. A little later two men visited Goodwin and he accompanied them outside to the stoop of the station house.

About 2:15 Smith noticed Goodwin was no longer on the stoop. He looked around outside but couldn't find him. Smith notified Officer Wade, who was assigned to patrol the area near the station house about Goodwin's absence, but he could not find him in the immediate area. Smith then got Roundsman Wilbur out of bed to help search.

At approximately 3 A.M., when Goodwin could still not be located, Smith went to Sgt. Richard Magan's room, who was also on reserve, and woke him. Magan remained in bed and told Smith that if he had to get up and take over the desk duty, he would have no choice but to bring charges against Goodwin. Smith returned to Magan's room twenty minutes later to inform Magan that Goodwin had still not been located.

At 3:30 Smith notified Captain Edward Carpenter, the commanding officer of the Fourth Precinct. At about 4:35 with the captain standing in front of the desk Goodwin walked into the station house under the influence of alcohol.

"Where have you been, John?" asked the captain. "Why did you leave the desk?"

"I was here all the time." Goodwin replied.

Carpenter shook his head. "No, you weren't John. I was here the whole time, and you weren't."

Because he could see Goodwin had been drinking Carpenter directed him to go upstairs to bed.

Carpenter began returning to his room, but Goodwin followed saying. "You think you're big stuff. You can't do any harm to me. I won't go to bed. I'm gonna stay right here where I belong." Three or four officers then forcibly persuaded Goodwin to go to bed.

At 7 A.M. the captain went to the backroom of the station house and spoke to Goodwin "John, where were you?"

"I was here." Goodwin still insisted

"No, you weren't," Carpenter said

No matter how hard the captain pressed him, Goodwin insisted he had gone no further than the stoop.

Sergeant Magan saw Goodwin in the back room around 8 A.M. Goodwin asked him what he should do, and Magan told him he should report sick, which he did at about 8 A.M. Later in the day Goodwin reported to the office of Police Surgeon Nammack at 29 Jefferson

Street. Dr. Nammack examined him and found him unfit for duty due to alcoholism. Nammack directed another uniformed patrolman to take Goodwin home.

...

On August 12, 1889, Dr. Nammack was present at the Fourth Precinct in Captain Carpenter's office when Goodwin and his wife, Isabella asked to speak to Carpenter. Goodwin wanted the captain to withhold the charges brought against him for being missing from the precinct on the 9th – he said the captain owed it to him for a reason he did not specify. Carpenter said there was nothing he could do.

Later that day, John and Isabella Goodwin visited the saloon/restaurant owned by Amelia Westphal. The establishment was located about a half block from the Fourth Precinct station house at 366 Pearl Street. When the Goodwin's entered at dinnertime, John was not in a sober condition. He engaged in a verbal dispute with Mrs. Westphal before roughly pushing her against an icebox.

On August 13th, John Goodwin was still on sick leave and had an appointment to visit Dr. Nammack at 1 PM. John wanted Isabella to get some air that day, so she accompanied him to his appointment. Because Isabella was due to give birth in a few weeks and had difficulty walking, John rented a horse and buggy from a stable on 78th Street before continuing downtown.

At the appointment with Dr, Nammack at 315 Second Avenue, the doctor found him unfit for duty and directed him to continue on sick leave. Goodwin then continued in the buggy downtown to pick up a fox terrier and a parrot that were being held for him. The dog was in a grocery store on Pearl Street and the bird was in a liquor store on the corner of Water and Dover Streets run by a man named Huyler.

John picked up the dog without incident and had at least one drink when he stopped at the liquor store to get the bird. When he returned to the buggy, he gave the bird to Isabella and continued driving the buggy. When they reached Oak and Pearl Streets Goodwin said the dog tried to eat the parrot, which Isabella held tightly in her arms. The dog got its feet tangled in the lace of Isabella's dress, so John gave her the reins so he could untangle the dog. The buggy ran into a truck, and Goodwin, Isabella, dog and bird were thrown out of the overturning buggy.

Goodwin hit his head on the pavement and landed on his wife, seriously injuring her and rendering her unconscious. Goodwin told onlookers to take his wife to the nearby Fourth Precinct station house while he momentarily tended to the buggy. When Goodwin entered the station house his wife was seated in a chair next to the station house desk being tended to by Sergeant Richard Magan.

Goodwin ran to his wife. "My poor wife" Goodwin cried as he ran to Isabella.

Magan caught him by the arm "John, allow me to care for your wife."

Goodwin was upset and said he would care for his own wife at which point Magan said he ought to lock Goodwin up for being drunk. Magan called several cops to take Goodwin into the back room, saying "You ought to get out of this business and resign."

At that moment Goodwin noticed Doorman Smith standing nearby. "Get out of here you son of a bitch – you put this job on me." The hostility Goodwin was displaying toward the Doorman was due to the fact that he blamed Smith for reporting him missing from the precinct on August 9th and the subsequent charges he received.

Sergeant Magan noticed that some of the people who had helped carry Isabella to the precinct were still inside the station house and were intently listening to Goodwin's rant. "John, don't talk that way here in front of these people." he warned.

Goodwin sneered at the sergeant. "You son of a bitch – he is one of your friends."

"I won't have you talk to me that way here." Magan said as he directed Goodwin to go to the back room to cool down.

Instead of obeying the sergeant's order, Goodwin rushed towards Smith and tried to attack him. Several officers, including Magan restrained him. Magan told him his behavior was out of line, and Goodwin again said, "You son of a bitch – he is one of your friends."

Magan then told several officers to bring Goodwin to the back room. When Smith walked to the back-room Goodwin had to be restrained from attacking him again.

When Magan returned to the desk area to continue his care of Isabella, he said to her, "This is a nice fix John has gotten into – upsetting his carriage and coming here drunk. If he is going to get out of this business, why doesn't he get out like a gentleman – if he is going to act like this the only thing he can do is resign."

Smith returned to the desk area and told Magan of the attempted second attack. Magan returned to the back room and told Goodwin he should resign.

"Why should I?" Goodwin responded.

Magan returned to the desk area and ordered several cops to lock Goodwin in a cell. The cops hesitated at locking up a brother officer, but when Magan threatened to charge them, Goodwin was taken to a cell. Magan told Goodwin he would keep him locked up overnight and send him to court in the morning if he did not resign.

While Sergeant Magan was in the back seeing that Goodwin was placed in a cell, Captain Carpenter returned to the station house from patrol. Isabella was still seated in the station house in great pain. She saw the captain and said, "John has gotten himself into trouble again."

The captain told Isabella to let the officers take her home, but she pleaded to see her husband. Carpenter escorted Isabella back to the cell and when they approached Goodwin he cried, "Oh for God's sake captain, let me out of here."

Carpenter said, "Johnny, you've got yourself in a pretty bad scrape. If I was you, I think I would resign."

Isabella said, "Do as the captain tells you. He has always been your friend."

Captain Carpenter released Goodwin from the cell and escorted him back to the front desk. Sergeant Magan had a letter of resignation prepared and told Goodwin to sign it. He refused and Magan threatened to put him back in the cell. Since it was the only way he would be released to care for his wife, Goodwin said he would sign the resignation under protest.

As he was about to sign the letter of resignation Goodwin said to Magan, "If I make trouble for you, it's your own fault." He then signed his name and began to write "under protest" underneath his name but Magan pulled the letter away before he completed the word "protest." Goodwin then departed with his wife.

Goodwin would not give up his shield because he believed he was still a member of the department. When leaving the station house Isabella told Magan that if Johnnie made trouble for him, it would be his own fault. [3]

Life was not easy for Isabella Goodwin. John launched a legal battle to get his job back, claiming that he was forced to resign under duress and that Sergeant Magan had committed forgery by writing "Roundsman" over the area under his signature where he had begun to write "Under Protest" before the paper was snatched away from him. But this legal struggle lasted for years, and Isabella still had to care for her children and provide for a family that included a husband with serious alcohol issues. Isabella couldn't have known for sure who was right, but she certainly supported her husband.

Isabella was thankful that they still had the income from the Willow Cottage restaurant they ran. On January 5, 1890, however, that income went up in smoke – literally.

Policeman Matthew Gounaud was patrolling on the cold, clear night at 23rd Street and Eleventh Avenue when he noticed flames playing around a stove pipe that ran through the wooden ceiling of the restaurant. The firemen were on hand in three minutes, but by that time the flames had spread to the lumber yard next to the restaurant setting the entire area ablaze. The flames made the area seem like daylight, and thousands of gawkers watched the ravaging of the Ernest Fincken and Son Manhattan Steam Kindling-Wood Yard along with A.W. Budlong, a dealer in pine and hardwood lumber. Also completely destroyed was the Goodwin's restaurant. Isabella's situation had just gone from bad to worse. As if her plight wasn't bad enough, a few days later while John was out, a police inspector came to her home and forcefully took John's shield and fire key when she refused to give them up voluntarily. [4]

John Goodwin's battle against his superiors became the "longest and most persistently fought litigation in the annals of the police department." During its six-year duration, the case went to the state supreme court. The newspapers overlooked his alcohol problems and celebrated John as a hero cop battling the corrupt system, especially when one of his claims was that he was being retaliated against for complaining about higher-ups ushering prostitutes to the stationhouse for their own enjoyment. During that time, John and Isabella had two more children, James and Marjorie.

Finally, after nearly six years John Goodwin was reinstated to the police department. Members of the department were shocked and surprised when Goodwin compromised on the amount of back pay he was due. The court ordered the police department to pay Goodwin $7,194.78 in back pay and costs. Goodwin accepted $5,000 back pay and $1,143.97 in costs, forfeiting about $900. Once reinstated, Goodwin was assigned to duty in the Tremont station house.

Goodwin's lawyer, Louis Grant, explained the reason for the compromise. "For nearly six years," he said, "the man has been fighting this case, and during that time he and his family have at times been in actual want. The decision of the general term was a godsend to him, yet he knew, and I knew that if the commissioners chose, they could fight the case further, and although the decision would be the same in the end, they might keep Goodwin off of the force for the next five of six months. He couldn't afford to wait that long under any circumstances and so he compromised with the commissioners, although he lost about $900 in doing it. Now, he's back at work and he is happy because he can hold his head up with any man in the department." [5]

Even though he was back on the job and had received his back pay, John Goodwin's problems did not simply vanish. Within months, he began acting strangely. He insisted a curse rested upon him. [6] On July 10, 1895 Goodwin was transferred from the Tremont station to the West 125th Street station. [7]

One day during November he arrived at the station house drunk to an extent that three policemen were required to corral him into a cell. The courts committed him to Bellevue Hospital for alcoholism. Commissioner Theodore Roosevelt ordered Goodwin examined by the Board of Surgeons, and even told the New York Times that it had been reported that Goodwin was insane. On December 11th, the trial began on three charges of intoxication. John Goodwin called eighteen witnesses—seventeen policemen from the 125th Street station and his wife, Isabella. One by one, they each got up and declared him insane. [8]

Before his trial was completed Acting Chief Conlin ordered Goodwin suspended again on December 30th after he was locked up by Acting Captain Grant for being drunk. Goodwin was in such bad condition from the effects of his prolonged spree, when arraigned for examination in Harlem Court, the hearing was postponed, and he was sent to Bellevue Hospital. [9]

John Goodwin never drew a sober breath again. A police surgeon found him on his bed, partly dressed and imagining that he saw people peeping through doors and windows. He died August 11, 1896, the deadliest day of the apocalyptic Heat Wave of 1896. The death was, for Isabella Goodwin, possibly a relief in some ways. Her husband had finally been swept into a more merciful oblivion. But in other respects, it was a disaster. In those days, there was no life insurance. She and her family could not live for long on the money John's fellow officers had fished from their pockets for the widow's collection, and the back pay had mainly been used to pay off the debts they had accumulated during the six years of the legal battle.

The restaurant and the police department were the only two institutions Isabella Goodwin had known during her adult life. The restaurant was gone, so, in 1896, she entered the police force through the only gate available for a woman at the time. [10]

Chapter 2: Matron

It was in 1845 when the American Female Reform Society fought for and won the right to install two police matrons at the Manhattan House of Detention, worryingly referred to as "The Tombs." This was a grime riddled hellhole, and it wasn't the last place as such where these female police matrons found themselves. Asylums followed, lawless places of sheer incompetence and indifference, but it marked a notable shift in attitudes. It was now thought that women should care for women.

Finally, in 1888 New York State passed legislation allowing New York City to appoint two matrons to each of its police stations. The law stated that not more than two respectable women should be appointed, who would be known as police matrons. Women thus appointed were to be recommended by at least 20 women of good standing in their community. Where only one matron was to be attached to a police station she had to reside within the station, or within a reasonable distance from it, and was to hold herself in readiness to respond to any call from the station at any hour day or night

In October 1888 neither New York City nor Brooklyn had hired matrons, citing the lack of money. The New York City police commissioners made a nominal effort by designating a specific police station where women would be confined. In Brooklyn, five precincts were designated as locations where females could be brought. There was no benefit in these designations because there were no matrons at these designated locations for females, and sometimes females had to be transported great distances under harsh traveling conditions to reach one of these facilities.

By summer of 1890 the law had been on the books for two years, but New York City had still refused to act. The law was permissive but not mandatory, meaning that a city was authorized to appoint matrons but not legally compelled to do so. Finally, in March 1892

Governor Hill signed into law a bill making it mandatory on the police commissioners to appoint matrons within three months.

The police board continued to drag its feet claiming lack of money. The commissioners also cited that a matron would not be free from insult by the policemen of the station houses. This was quite a commentary on the quality of the policemen because "insult" during that era was a code for rape or assault. The commissioner most notably against the appointment of matrons was John Richard Voorhis. He said the $30,000 a year it would cost to employ matrons was too high. Voorhis also noted that ninety percent of all females arrested were from the lowest and most depraved strata of human life and did not require the delicate handling of a female. The commissioners also said that there were already women employed in the station houses who performed many tasks matrons would be called upon to do. These women were paid by the policemen themselves and not under the control of the police board. Yet, rule 526 of the police board directed these women to be called upon to search female prisoners under certain circumstances.

The pressure to hire matrons continued and finally paid off when in May 1891 an examination for police matron was conducted. The 28 women tested had to answer questions such as what to do during childbirth and what to do with a drunken woman. In addition, the candidates were required to do certain simple arithmetic problems and to read out loud from a newspaper to an examiner. One of the math problems required candidates to show how ten prisoners could be placed in nine cells. Salary for the post of matron could be no less than the lowest salary paid to a policeman, then $1,000 per year.

Some 140 applicants had been initially received by the police board, but the board whittled the number down when it decided not to appoint any woman to a matron's place if she was less than thirty years old or more than forty-five. Since twenty of the initial applicants had ranged in age from 21-29 and twenty others ranged from 46-70, they were all eliminated. Several eminent women had been invited to help the Civil Service Board in administering the exam. Eventually, a list of the twenty highest candidates on the exam would be certified and the police board would select its police matrons from that list. For a start, eight stations were designated to receive females – meaning the first target was to hire eight matrons. The first four matrons started work in New York City police stations on October 5, 1891, and by 1899 the city employed 61 police matrons.

Less than three weeks after the first four matrons started work, Josephine Lowell, one of the State Charity Commissioners, wrote to the police commissioners complaining that the work expected of the matrons was excessive. On the day shift matrons worked ten-hour days, and on the night shift they worked fourteen hours. In addition, these women were required to climb the stairs around thirty times each day. Lowell urged the hiring of more matrons. In reply to the letter, Commissioner Voorhis stated that matrons were not expected to do any more work than doormen of the station houses and that Lowell's letter "bore out the position taken by the board at the beginning that the work was too hard for women." [11]

Regardless of the police board's opinion, women were entering the police department to stay. New York Governor David B. Hill agreed with the Women's Prison Association of New York that women would have to perform the searches of arrested women from then on, watch them in their cells, and bring them water. But it could no longer just be one of the officer's wives, called from her home when available. And it certainly could no longer be a man. The Departmental Civil Service Board, started a year before Isabella Goodwin's employ, hired officers based on merit, as opposed to the bribes they paid. [12]

For Commissioner Theodore Roosevelt, bringing women into the department was gold. What better way to endear oneself than to promote radical new ideas that shook the establishment to the core, striking at the heart of traditional policing roles. In 1891, he went a step further by transforming the duty of the female police matron to deal with female crime victims, sex crimes and cases involving children, arguing it was of paramount importance to rid New York of this scourge. Women lined up as far as the eye could see. The women of old New York had mobilized and soon, Isabella would be one of the legions coming to protect the poor and downtrodden, forgotten and uncared for.

Isabella was close to becoming one of those poor and downtrodden. She was in trouble. With four children crammed into a tiny apartment in a part of town less desirable than a filth-strewn slum, Isabella needed work – and fast. Her late husband had provided all the inspiration she needed. She was fascinated by the world of policing, but it was dangerous with children and only her mother to care for them. Nevertheless, she applied to become a police matron.

Isabella was an ideal candidate. The New York Police Department was eager to bring more and more women onboard, and even though the job was administered through civil service rules, the authorities actively sought out widows. This was a golden public relations move for the police department. Look at us! We are hiring women, and better yet, women down-on-their-luck, struggling with no money and no income. Here we come to give these women work and a salary. It did the job. The New York Police Department never looked better.

Goodwin studied, then reported to the exam board for physical and written tests. She handed the board the reference letters from twenty "women of good standing." Despite her troubles, Goodwin probably collected those letters with relative ease. For years when she was a child, her parents, Anna J. Monteith and the late James Harvey Loghry, owned a restaurant and hotel down on Canal Street, between Thompson and Laurens. Their business was reputable enough to earn listings in both Trow's New York City Directory and Goulding's. The friendships made through their household lodger, a Tammany Hall mascot and vote counter for the First District, Harry F. Bezant, might have provided some additional credentials. Seven years earlier, Isabella's older sister Margaret had married Julius T. Tunstall, a well-established printer and a master of the Grand Lodge of Masons, placing her in the right sort of company. And two years after that, her younger sister, Nellie, married a well-off wool merchant, again the sort of middle-class arrival putting her among "women of good standing." The police matron's essay question when Isabella took the test was, "Do you favor the consolidation of territory known as Greater New York?" The newspapers at the time resounded with arguments for and against. [13]

Predictably, she aced the exam. Isabella was intelligent and logically minded. She could figure out puzzles the likes of which baffled so many more. Isabella was hired as a matron in May of 1896 and assigned to the Mercer Street station house. Isabella was given a new uniform and shield, the uniform being a tailor-made blue serge with a tight-fitting waist and a skirt to the shoe tops. Her shield was smaller than a patrolman's.

At once, she was thrust into the dark world of jail matron, Theodore Roosevelt himself shook her hand when she was appointed, the very same man who would later become President. This wasn't much, but it was something. For what was one of the hardest jobs in America at the time, Isabella was paid $1,000 a year, around $36,000 in today's money. For the police, this was the lowest of the low. No other officers were paid this little, but Isabella didn't care. It paid the bills and most importantly, it kept her children alive. They and her elderly mother were all she had left.

For a few years Isabella performed the duties of a typical police matron. She looked out for the welfare of women who were brought into the station for a variety of reasons. She made sure the women were kept separate from the male prisoners and were treated well by male officers. She kept an eye on female prisoners who were suicide risks and found shelter for children whose mothers were in jail. But matron work was physically demanding and took place in testing environments.

Matrons spent long shifts, during the day and overnight, in poorly maintained, uncomfortable stationhouses. Here they searched the bodies of female detainees, dealt with intoxicated women and rough sleepers, and managed overcrowded cells. In addition to these tasks, they tended to children who were temporarily and permanently lost by their parents, as well as to sick women awaiting medical attention. The laborious nature of this work made it unappealing to middle-class women. The introduction of matrons also coincided with an increase in the number of women arrested by the NYPD. Perhaps policemen felt more comfortable detaining women with the knowledge that they would enter a matron's custody. From these beginnings, women's presence furthered the ability of municipal police to regulate female residents. [14]

Life was extremely hard for Isabella. She had just one day off a month but spent each of those days taking her children to the park to spend as much time as she could with them. But Isabella was no ordinary matron. Even then, in the early days of a career that would last many years, it was obvious she had a knack for the job. Her bosses sent her undercover to investigate crimes all whilst her mother watched her children. She enjoyed the taste of these new assignments she received once in a while, and she turned out to be a brilliant undercover cop.

Most matrons spent their police careers within the stationhouse, but a small number of opportunistic matrons sought new duties, at first within the precinct by assisting on investigations involving women and children in police custody, drawing upon perceived feminine expertise. In the 1910s, the NYPD increasingly relied upon matrons' sleuthing skills to resolve a range of cases, particularly those affecting women. Practicalities partially inspired this system, as men could not convincingly pose as victims of certain crimes. Additionally, as a minority presence on the police, women aroused less suspicion; their femininity masked their state-given regulatory power. [15]

After Isabella had been working as a matron for about six years, something happened that became a turning point in her life. The captain needed a woman to go undercover to capture some people who were running an illegal gambling establishment – betting on horse races. The business was operating in a poolroom that was open only to women patrons. The police suspected the illegal activities were taking place there, but they needed proof. They needed a woman to get into the poolroom and gather evidence. The captain asked Isabella to help.

Isabella went undercover to see what she could learn. She spent time in the neighborhood where the poolroom was located. She made it known that she was interested in gambling, and soon she met a woman who took her into the pool hall. "What do you know about horses?" one of the women running the place asked her.

"Sleepyhead looks good to me," Isabella responded. And she placed a $5 bet on a horse named Sleepyhead.

Within a short time, Isabella had gathered evidence to bring charges against the women. But because she was only a matron, she did not have arrest powers. She gave the information to the male officers, and they lost no time in raiding the poolroom.

"My, I never saw such excitement in my life when I heard the police battering down the doors," Isabella recalled. "The women began to scream and run around like hens without their heads." She later described the scene. "These gambling ladies hadn't a drop of sporting blood left."

The arresting officers rounded up the women and loaded them into the patrol wagon for a ride to the station. Isabella never blew her cover, managing to slip away from the wagon before it headed to the station. Since the gambling women never knew Isabella had been working with the police, she was free to participate in future undercover assignments.

Isabella's poolroom assignment showed her supervisors that she could be valuable to them in investigative work. She was ready to do more, and they were willing to give her additional opportunities. Her appearance often worked to her advantage. She was described as attractive and gracious. Her bright brown eyes and quiet friendliness of manner were her best disguises. Criminals didn't expect a woman, especially one who looked like Isabella – middle aged and respectable. She loved the undercover work and became depressed whenever she had to return to matron duties. In 1912, Isabella would not be depressed for very long. [16]

Chapter 3: The Great Taxicab Robbery

As 1912 began Isabella was still officially a police matron, but she was enjoying her assignment with the Detective Bureau where she was given the opportunity to perform the undercover investigative assignments that she enjoyed, and at which she excelled.

On Thursday, February 15, 1912, Isabella's eyes widened as she scanned the headline of a New York evening newspaper. Between ten and eleven o'clock that morning two messengers were sent in a taxicab from the East River National Bank, at Broadway and Third street, to draw $25,000 in currency from the Produce Exchange National Bank, at Broadway and Beaver Street, in the downtown financial district, and deliver the money to a bank uptown. This transfer of money had been made several times a week for so long a period without danger or loss that the messengers were unarmed. One of them, Wilbur F. Smith, was an old man who had been in the service of the bank thirty-five years, and the other was a mere boy, named Frank Worell, sixteen years old.

The taxicab driver, named Geno Montani, seemed almost a trusted employee, too, for he operated two cabs from a stand near the bank, and was frequently called upon for such trips.

At the bank the messengers presented checks for $25,000 and received three thousand $5 bills and one thousand $10 bills, some new and some old. Those they put into a brown leather telescopic bag. [17]

While the cab was returning uptown through Church Street with the money, five men suddenly closed in upon it. They had been waiting there about half an hour. When the taxicab turned the corner the five jumped into the street and surrounded the taxicab. According to the taxi driver's story, a sixth man forced him to reduce speed by stumbling in front of the vehicle.

Immediately two men on each side of the cab opened the doors. Two assailants were boosted in and quickly beat the messengers into insensibility, while their two helpers ran along on the sidewalk. The two messengers were being struck repeated blows on the head with blackjacks. They fought back, but the older man soon fell in a daze to the floor of the cab, and a few more blows put the boy out of commission. The fifth man climbed onto the seat beside the driver, held a revolver to his ribs, and ordered him to drive fast or be killed. This fellow seemed to be familiar with automobiles and threatened the driver when he tried to reduce speed. That was a busy part of the city, yet nobody on the sidewalks seemed to notice anything out of the ordinary. The cab dodged vehicles, going at high speed for several blocks.

At Park Place and Church Street Montani brought the cab to a stop. "Now, don't make a sound and don't make a move. That's all you have to do," was the final warning of the holdup man, as he jumped from the driver's seat at the same time that his companions in the taxi opened the doors and jumped out, one of them carrying the brown bag with the $25,000. They ran quickly to a black automobile without a license number which was waiting for them, and in a few moments were gone.

That was the substance of the story. As Isabella folded the newspaper, she knew police headquarters would be in a state of chaos. The police could initially only gather information chiefly from the driver, because the two bank employees had been attacked so suddenly and viciously that they lost consciousness in a moment. When the driver looked inside his cab after the crime, he said he saw them both lying senseless and bleeding. They could give no description of the assailants. The elderly messenger, Smith, was seriously hurt, and he was taken in an ambulance to the Hudson Street Hospital. Young Worell's injuries were not so severe. His wounds were dressed, and he was taken to police headquarters, with the taxi driver.

Eyewitnesses were found who had seen men loitering in the neighborhood where the cab was boarded shortly before the crime, but their descriptions were not very useful. That night, thousands of New

Yorkers like Isabella read the published accounts of the crime in the newspapers under great black headlines, and on the following morning every news item of a criminal nature was grouped in the same part of the papers to prove that the city had entered one of its sensational "waves of crime." And for more than a week the public read criticism and denunciation of the police force.

The newspapers charged that red tape had brought the police department to such a low state that young detectives had no idea what a real criminal looked like, and urged the restoration of the old system, with its picturesque "line-up."

In the days of Inspector Tommy Byrnes, a legendary figure in NYPD history, when practically all the banking of the city was done around Wall Street, the police established a "dead line" beyond which criminals were supposed not to operate. [18]

The "dead line" was the invention of Byrnes, who announced it on March 12, 1880, the day he became New York City's Chief of Detectives. Chief Byrnes, who had a force of 28 men to investigate crime among two million inhabitants, reasoned that the city's worst burglars, robbers and fraud artists were focused on Lower Manhattan's financial district and its nearby jewelry district.

Chief Byrnes decreed that henceforth, the police would observe an invisible line drawn along Fulton Street, above the financial district's northern edge. Any known criminal found below that line would be arrested on sight, whether he was acting suspiciously or not. The expression "dead line" was thought to have come from the Civil War, when Confederate guards at Andersonville Prison in Georgia were said to have drawn a line several feet inside the walls; prisoners stepping beyond that line were immediately shot.

"Byrnes was willing to take it for granted that cracksmen and stickup men did not visit the financial district to study the bond market or to purchase diamond studs," an article in The New York Times said in 1924. "He felt that their presence among some of the greatest temptations in the world was as open to as much suspicion as the visits of a cat to a bird store."

Because arrests below the dead line placed a premium on quick identification, Chief Byrnes established the first "mug file" for detectives, with sketches and, later, photos of wrongdoers, along with other personal information in a virtual encyclopedia of bad guys. The chief was not immune to benefiting occasionally from the gratitude of merchants and bankers. He testified in 1894 that he had made $350,000 through shrewd use of their advice. His salary during much of the time was $2,000. [19]

Without enforcement of the dead line it was feared that crooks who were known to experienced detectives could roam the financial district at will. The detectives said their hands were tied because under an order issued by Mayor Gaynor, they were not allowed to pick up professional thieves unless there was a charge against them. The lineup of thieves at police headquarters in the morning had been abolished, and most veteran detectives cynically noted that many of the younger detectives wouldn't know a crook with a reputation unless he introduced himself. These veteran sleuths told a story at police headquarters of two detectives walking on Wall Street when two old time crooks greeted them.

"Hello, lieutenant," said one of the crooks, saluting. "Ta- ta, you can't do a thing to us. No more picking up these days because the mayor says you can't. You've got nothing on us, and we say goodbye to you." [20]

In its day, the "dead line" was real enough, but it was not necessarily an ideal police measure, and the growth of the city eventually made it a mere memory, living only in newspaper tradition. By 1912, banking extended as far north as Central Park, and millions upon millions of dollars were being carried about daily by people of every sort.

After a week passed with no apparent progress being made on the case, public sentiment regarding the police transitioned from outrage to humor, and the city ventured to joke about the case. One reason for the ridicule and mocking was that Lt. Faurot, the NYPD fingerprint expert photographed many prints found on the cab. Unfortunately, the crime scene had not been secured by the police and many curious onlookers had opened the doors of the cab while it sat outside headquarters unprotected. [21]

At an elaborate public dinner one night, among other topical effects, a dummy taxicab suddenly scooted out before the guests, held up a dummy police commissioner, took his watch, and scooted away again. The diners laughed, and that was fairly representative of the town, which was now ready to have its joke about the crime, too. Had there never been any further action by the police, the case would have quietly dropped out of sight with the only lasting memory being the ineptitude of the police department. But fortunately, there was police action. The action started with a burly, genial man, sitting in a big office at Police Headquarters. The office was that of the Second Deputy Police Commissioner, and the man was the Deputy Commissioner himself, George S. Dougherty.

George Dougherty had nearly twenty-five years' experience in criminal work in New York, and over the whole country. Until his appointment by Mayor Gaynor in May 1911, he was connected with the Pinkerton organization. Bank and financial crimes had long been his specialty, so the taxicab case fell right into his own province. He knew the ways of forgers, bank sneaks, swindlers, burglars and safe crackers, and was personally acquainted with most of the criminals in those lines in and out of prison.

New Yorkers were fascinated by the newspaper reports of the daring robbery pulled off in broad daylight on a crowded city street in the heart of the Financial District. Dougherty was not nearly as enthralled. He was in charge of the NYPD's five-hundred-man detective branch, and he intended to capture the perpetrators before a spate of copycats utilizing getaway cars became a common occurrence.

Dougherty knew that the police would have a tough time catching such robbers, because the department only had six automobiles in its entire fleet. Deputy Commissioner Dougherty dominated the story. The taxicab robbers were eventually caught by his methods, plans and supervision, backed by the splendid teamwork of the men under him – and one crucial female.

Sixty detectives were immediately called into the case. Five of them went down to the scene of the robbery, with orders to work there until further notice. They made a thorough search of the neighborhood, following the route taken by Montani's taxicab, and questioning merchants, newsdealers, porters, truckmen and other persons likely to have information as eyewitnesses. They went through the streets that may had been taken by the escaping robbers and worked over the whole ground. This search through one of the busiest sections of New York in a busy hour, amid the excitement created by the crime, appeared like hopeless business, but it yielded important results. Other detectives searched garages for the black automobile without a license number in which the robbers were reported to have gotten away. Four uniformed policemen on beats along the route taken by the taxicab were questioned. But the most important work of the first day centered at Police Headquarters where a conference was held by Deputy Commissioner Dougherty and his assistants, and in the examination of Geno Montani, the taxicab driver.

The attendees at the conference judged the robbery strictly as a piece of workmanship. Names of known bank criminals were brought up, one by one, and details gone over. It soon became clear that none of the men identified with bank crime were likely to have the brains, skill or organization to plan and execute so complicated a robbery.

The criminals in this robbery had known the habits of the bank in conveying cash uptown. They knew the route and were aware that the security was only an elderly man and a sixteen-year-old boy, both unarmed. They had boarded the cab at the best point, and evidently made arrangements for stopping it. There was teamwork in every detail. It showed marked insight, for instance, to provide additional men to boost each assailant in at the doors. For young Worell, the bank employee, had made a plucky attempt to shove his robber out and shut the door, and might have succeeded had there not been an outside man. Robberies were committed under exciting conditions. They sometimes failed because criminals would get cold feet. That outside man was there not only to help his "slugger" into the cab, but to force him in if he tried to back away and make certain he did his work. Whoever planned such details, it was agreed at the conference, possessed more cunning than the ordinary bank criminal.

When Montani, the taxicab driver, arrived at Police Headquarters, he was willing to talk, and seemed anxious to help the police in every way. He knew suspicion might be directed toward him but did not resent that. He talked like a man confident of the truth of his story, and certain that he would be found blameless.

Montani was from the northern part of Italy, about 30 years old, five feet six inches tall, rather stout and thick set, with a very dark complexion. The striking feature of his countenance was his large, intelligent brown eyes. Deputy Commissioner Dougherty found himself thinking of Napoleon in connection with Montani.

The first examination lasted all afternoon, with a break when Montani went out to lunch with Dougherty. Hundreds of questions were asked bearing on the robbery, the appearance of the criminals, and Montani's past and personal affairs. The story was gone over again and again, and different questioners relieved each other, yet the taxicab man never lost his temper or patience and did not contradict himself in any important details. Montani had been in the United States since the age of twelve. He had a wife and two children and was the owner of two taxicabs operated from a stand at a hotel near the bank, whose money he regularly carried. He had owned three cabs but lost one through business reverses. Starting originally as a truckman for a salvage company, his ambition and intelligence had won him such confidence that this company lent him money to set up trucking for himself. Still more ambitious, he had become a taxicab proprietor. Through the trickery of an ill-chosen partner, however, he had lost some of his savings. He seemed a little bitter about this, and it was a circumstance not likely to escape an expert police examiner, for the loss of money through fraud, coupled with temptation, could often be the starting point in crime. Montani's former employers spoke highly of his character when questioned by detectives. He gave the names of chauffeurs who had worked for him lately, and of businesspeople who knew him, and careful investigation failed to disclose any suspicious circumstances.

Montani quickly won over the newspaper men—so much so that, when he was discharged in court a few days later for apparent lack of evidence, the newspapers criticized the police for having held him at all. And yet, before that first night, Montani himself, largely through simple answers to questions, had become so involved that there was ground for holding him under arrest.

Montani had slowed down his cab at the point where the robbers boarded it. He said that an old man had suddenly got in front, and he had reduced speed to avoid running over him. But detectives along the route found eyewitnesses who had seen the robbers board the cab, and who could testify that there had been nobody in front of the vehicle.

Both of his cabs had stood in line near the bank that morning, the one driven by himself being second, and the other, in the charge of an employee, was first. When the call came from the bank, Montani answered it himself out of his turn, sending the other cab uptown, as he explained, to have some tires vulcanized.

Montani said that as soon as the robbers left his cab, he had raised a cry for help. But eyewitnesses were found who denied this. Instead of running north after the robbers' automobile when he had taken a policeman aboard his cab, he ran south, away from it. This action, he maintained, was taken under orders from the policeman. But the policeman denied that.

Interest centered in the mysterious black automobile without a license number. For, though Montani was an experienced driver, and his replies to other questions showed that he had seen both the rear and the side of that car, he was unable to tell its make. Meanwhile, it was learned that three men had hurriedly boarded an elevated train near the scene of the robbery shortly after, not waiting for change from a quarter. The ticket-seller was unable to describe them but connected them with the robbery when he heard about it.

Dougherty became convinced that Montani was involved, but he had no way to prove it. Without evidence, the courts forced him to set the cabbie free. Montani was discharged, with comment by the court upon the flimsiness of the police case. There was one striking discrepancy in the evidence presented at that examination. He still insisted that he had stopped his cab because an old man had got in front of it, but this was denied by a witness.

Montani went free, and was jubilant, calling on Dougherty the next morning to thank him. But from the moment he left court until he was arrested again Montani never got out of sight of the Police Department. Montani stopped in at Police Headquarters repeatedly, accompanied by his unseen shadowers. He professed to be anxious to furnish further information he could recall, and Dougherty chatted with him cordially, leading him to believe that he no longer rested under the slightest suspicion.

In reality, Montani had planned the crime, recruited the crew, laid out every detail in his mind, and arranged his story beforehand. He expected to be arrested and said so. He admitted that there were inconsistencies in his story but hoped to clear them up. He had discussed the crime with his crew and had not been seen in their company. So, having settled on his story, Montani stuck to it without variation under every form of pressure. The other members of the gang forgot what they had arranged as their defense, or departed from it, or broke down and confessed, but not Montani. He alone went to trial and stuck to his story until the end.

Dougherty came to the department with a reliable stable of informants he had developed during his Pinkerton days. One of his stool pigeons contacted him with information about an acquaintance he knew as Eddie Collins. Informants were not always reliable, nor always possessed useful information, but Dougherty was desperate for information, and this informant had the first real clue.

The informant said that Collins had stopped by his boardinghouse to pick up another resident whom he identified as Collins's sweetheart, Annie Hull, aka "Swede Annie." He also saw Collins flash a large wad of cash to impress her. Police distributed photographs of "Swede Annie" and her boyfriend, whose real name was Eddie Kinsman, among railroad workers on the theory that they had already fled the city. A conductor recalled having seen the couple board a train in Peekskill bound for Albany. Dougherty sent detectives to the state capital to make inquiries. Soon afterward the police caught a second break when they talked to Swede Annie's landlady and learned that Hull had her belongings transferred to another boardinghouse on the West Side shortly before she checked out. It was also learned that a woman known as "Myrtle Hoyt," an intimate of Annie's, had moved to the lower West Side rooming house, taking Annie's trunk with her, as though Annie expected to return to the city.

Dougherty knew the key to this investigation would be to get information from Swede Annie. He needed to get someone inside that boarding house who could endear herself to Swede Annie and extract critical information from her in a short period of time. In other words, he needed a "roper" – someone to help get suspected criminals into the police net. In an instant Dougherty had the solution. He needed Isabella Goodwin.

The boarding house where Swede Annie's belongings had been brought to was run by a Mrs. Sullivan. Dougherty visited Mrs. Sullivan and after talking to her for a short time he decided to take a chance and let her in on his planned operation. He made the right decision. Mrs. Sullivan proved to be a wholesome, hard-working landlady, keeping a house that sheltered occasional suspicious characters, but was entirely honest herself. She was also willing to furnish information about her lodgers. "Sure, it's a good deal I know about that Collins, as he calls himself," she said, "and mighty little that's good."

It seemed that about two weeks earlier Collins had offered to pay the landlady if she would appear in a Brooklyn court and testify to the good character of a criminal named Molloy, who was being held for trial on a charge of robbery. Collins told her she would be paid fifteen to twenty dollars for appearing as a character witness.

"And do you think I'd take the stand and perjure myself swearing for a man I never heard of?" asked the indignant landlady.

Several days later, while she was putting some laundry into Collins' bureau drawer the landlady said she caught sight of two blackjacks. She asked Collins what he was doing with such weapons, and he told her he used them in business. Dougherty nearly fell over when Mrs. Sullivan continued to say that Collins told her that he knew a gang that was planning to rob a taxicab that carried money uptown to a bank every week. Mrs. Sullivan said she told him that he would end up in jail for a long time, but he shook his head and said it would be an easy job because they had fixed it with the taxi driver.

Early in the evening Mrs. Isabella Goodwin arrived at the boarding house with Deputy Commissioner Dougherty in tow, carrying her belongings. Mrs. Goodwin was "planted" as the landlady's "sister," who had come from Montreal to live with her and help in the housework until she could find a position in New York. As the Deputy Commissioner struggled with her bags, Dougherty grumbled a little about her stinginess in refusing to pay an expressman to bring her bundle, and then took his departure, explaining that the train had been late, and the baby was not well, and his wife, Aggie, would be worried about him, and so forth. Goodwin was aware of the danger she could be in while living among men and women who would not hesitate in using a knife or pistol if they dreamed a spy was in their midst, but she never hesitated in accepting the assignment. [22]

Mrs. Goodwin established herself in a room at the rear of the basement, close to the room occupied by Myrtle Hoyt, the woman who had brought Swede Annie's belongings to the boarding house. Isabella then went to work keeping her eyes and ears open as she went about the housework, slipping out to report when she had any information, and receiving instructions. Outside surveillance on this house was conducted from an empty store across the street. Goodwin was directed to report to Dougherty every night by code over the telephone. Everything with Dougherty was numbered and coded. The names of suspects were never mentioned or written out. [23]

When Isabella left her home to begin the assignment, she told her 19-year-old daughter Margaret, whose one ambition was to be a detective like her mother, that she would be busy on a case. She telephoned every day (not in code), but did not tell Margaret where she was or what she was doing. [24]

One day after Isabella began working at the boardinghouse, Swede Annie checked in. Over the next several days Goodwin worked to gain her confidence. Throughout the operation, Isabella wore a plain, dark, rather shabby suit, old shoes and an outdated hat, taking great care not to look too neat. She didn't want to look to anxious to talk to people and did whatever work she was asked to do although she grumbled a little and didn't always perform quality work. Isabella swept and scrubbed and made beds, washed dishes and answered the door, and slept in a wretched little dark hole and ate leftovers. The living conditions weren't pleasant.

Swede Annie was the present girlfriend of Eddie Kinsman, who was known also as Eddie Collins and Eddie the Boob. Myrtle Hoyt was his past sweetheart, so Goodwin obtained her facts by cultivating friendly relations with the rival women. She especially worked on the jealousy of Myrtle Hoyt. [25]

In a very short time Isabella became the confidante of each woman. They didn't mind talking to servants when they felt hysterically in need of an outburst, and Isabella didn't make the mistake of saying too much and though she was sympathetic she didn't react to show that anything she heard was of any importance. [26]

Isabella had to murder the English language during the operation, and she had to be very careful in asking questions. Another difficulty was inventing excuses to slip out to send her coded messages to Dougherty each night. [27]

A few days into the operation Swede Annie came back after an out-of-town trip. She looked quite glamorous in a new hat and suit. Isabella learned that Eddie had purchased Annie's new clothes in a store in Albany. She got the name of the store owner and passed it on to Dougherty. The clothier confirmed that a man of Eddie's description had bought the clothes and was "shedding money like a canary does feathers in the molting season."

Isabella also kept her ear on the door to the room that Annie shared with Hoyt. Meanwhile Dougherty's men followed leads that took them to Boston, Chicago, and Memphis.

On February 25th, Isabella struck gold. Swede Annie and Myrtle got into a huge shouting match resulting in Myrtle storming out of the boarding house. Isabella seized the opportunity and went right to work. Slowly she slid her way to the open door of Swede Annie's room. She could see Annie was still clearly fuming inside.

"What's wrong?" Isabella asked bravely in her 'Irish' lilt.

By the time Swede Annie had stopped talking, Isabella had her man. It was Eddie the Boob. He was behind the Taxi Bandit heist. She got him!

"Eddie the Boob turned the trick, alright," Swede Annie said. After spilling the beans Annie left to soothe her woes with a drink and a late-night shopping spree, returning to the house later that night in a fancy outfit and flashing a giant wad of cash. "I'm moving out!" she told Isabella with a drunken volume the entire house could hear. She was going to California, to a nice big house by the sea from the deeds of ill-gotten gains. Isabella had nailed it. They were going to be at Grand Central Station in the morning. As soon as Annie had dozed off in a drunken stupor, Isabella was outside sending the coded information to Dougherty. [28]

This was all the detectives needed to move in. Kinsman was arrested in Grand Central Station at half-past eleven in the morning, with Swede Annie. They were about to set out for Boston. There was little honor among the thieves, as Kinsman and Annie quickly implicated others, including Geno Montani, the cab driver.

The day after the arrests, Isabella was called into the police commissioner's office. When she spoke to reporters at headquarters, Isabella seemed self-assured, and confessed only to being a little tired. "It was the most interesting and exciting case I ever worked on," she admitted. "I was delighted when Commissioner Dougherty gave me the appointment.

Isabella had been with the department for 16-years but had been detailed as a detective for only about a year and a half. A great deal of her work had been the detection of fortune tellers and fake healers. The former included those who practiced with the crystal ball, the tarot cards and tea leaves, with handwriting, with palm-reading and with unadorned prophesy. In the hundreds of cases she worked she smiled in noting that she was never told the truth about her past life.

She said the faith healers were a stupid lot. One man completely cured her of stuttering, a problem she never had. She also said she investigated cases of licensed or unlicensed doctors who were suspected of performing illegal operations. She pretended to be a patient, and when it was sufficiently established that they were ready to treat her, she put them off for a day and returned with a warrant. Of course, she admitted her work was dangerous. She was never taken for a detective, but there was always a chance of being recognized which increased the longer she continued working. [29]

When Isabella recalled her role in the events, she admitted, "My flesh creeps sometimes – for these robbers were desperate men. I guess my life wouldn't have been worth much if they had suspected."

Deputy Commissioner Dougherty lavished praise on Isabella Goodwin and noted that the police matron had won her way into the detective bureau because of the work she did in rounding up fortunetellers. Dougherty explained that it was Isabella who obtained valuable evidence, evidence so important that it sent the deputy commissioner hustling around the city in an automobile late on Sunday and resulted in the arrests at Grand Central. [30]

Police Commissioner Waldo also noted that Mrs. Goodwin did very important work in the case. He also said that it was on information supplied by her that the male detectives arrested Edward Kinsman, who made the first confession, and enabled the police to round up the entire gang.

Commissioner Waldo was anxious to recognize the services of Isabella in a substantial way. He conceived the idea of promoting her to be a regular detective and asked the corporation counsel to look up the law. The law provided that the commissioner could promote any member of the police department. Mrs. Goodwin had been a member of the department since 1896, when she was made a matron at a salary of $1000 a year. [31] Commissioner Waldo informed Isabella that he was promoting her to detective. Isabella's new position meant her salary would more than double – from $1000 to $2,250 per year. Newspapers across the country reported on her status as the first municipal woman detective in the world. [32]

To say Isabella was pleased with the promotion would be putting it mildly. And she wasn't the only person happy with her newly elevated position. The opinion of her fellow male sleuths was that she deserved all she got. [33]

Geno Montani was the only member of the gang who did not fold and confess. He went to trial, was convicted and sentenced to 10-18 years in prison. Eddie Kinsman, Eugene Splaine, Robert Delio, James Pasquale, Joseph Lamb, Matteo Arbrano, and Jess Albrazzo pled guilty and received sentences of between two and seven years. Swede Annie Hull was held as a material witness but was not charged with the crime.

Chapter 4: The Detective

Several months after the fanfare from the taxicab robbery and subsequent arrests had become a distant flickering light in the city's collective memory, a newspaper advertisement appeared for a certain remarkable professor, who for the sum of one dollar agreed to tell people the occupation best fitted to them, to remove all evil influences and to reveal the names of their enemies. This advertisement was carefully clipped from the newspaper by a small, dark-haired woman with hazel eyes in a downtown office and pasted into a large book which stood on the top of a roll-top desk, after which she wrote the address in a tiny leather notebook. At the same time, on a crowded, bustling street on the Lower East Side, an immigrant woman who was the proud proprietor of a small grocery store clipped the same advertisement from the paper and stuffed it hurriedly into her handbag just before her husband came into the store to begin his morning's work.

A month later the immigrant woman was shown into the downtown office of NYPD Inspector Daniel "Honest Dan" Costigan. The veteran policeman's nickname was a commentary on the times. During the late 19th and early 20th centuries, corruption was rampant in the police department and there were numerous stories of police captains and inspectors who had become wealthy through graft. After many years on the force Costigan lived in a small apartment and had little money. Observers came to the conclusion that with such little personal wealth, he must be honest.

Honest Dan introduced the immigrant woman to Isabella Goodwin. Seated in a small straight-backed chair, the woman reached into her handbag and offered Isabella the professor's ad. Isabella opened her leather notebook and gazed at the two identical ads as the woman began the story of a swindle the pathos of which was not lost in its revelations of ignorance and superstition. Isabella sat silent, occasionally taking notes and asking questions when the thread of the story became difficult to follow.

The immigrant woman and her husband had been admitted at Ellis Island five years earlier. The husband, who by trade was a marble-worker, had secured a place in a small town in Pennsylvania, where he had been paid ten dollars a week. For this he polished marble underwater, which in winter, when there was ice, caused his feet to crack open and bleed, and his wife kept the house. After a year of this they had saved enough money to take them to New York where the husband obtained a job at twenty-five dollars a week. This was indeed a luxurious salary, but instead of increasing their standard of living, the couple still lived as frugally as possible and saved their money.

When they had fifteen hundred dollars in the bank, they bought a grocery store. The husband continued with his job while the woman worked in the store. The business was profitable and soon the woman was able to pay the small mortgage on the store and had thirty-five hundred dollars in the bank. The couple was on the verge of buying a chicken farm, selling the grocery store and moving to the country when the professor's alluring advertisement attracted her attention, and she was determined to seek his advice

For the sum of twenty-five dollars the professor removed an evil influence over the woman, told her the names of several persons who were jealous of her, and advised her not to buy the chicken farm. Instead, he explained she should invest her money in stocks, as the stars showed that this would be her most successful line, and he related numerous instances of individuals who had invested in various stocks under his direction who were now riding in motor cars and sending their children to college.

The woman was so thoroughly convinced that she mortgaged the grocery store to get more investment funds so that she could surprise her husband with the enormous returns on her investment. When she turned over the money to the professor, he presented her with impressive looking documents bearing gold seals, describing mining stock which had never been heard of by anyone but the professor. Then suddenly and inconspicuously, the professor left town. Any hope the couple had was now in the hands of Isabella Goodwin.

Isabella did not want the professor to know the police were on the case, so she borrowed some of the script from the taxicab robbery investigation by disguising herself as a maid and getting a job in the home next to the office the professor had been using. From this vantage point she discovered that the professor employed a doctor constantly while he was in the city, and Isabella was able to learn the name of this doctor. Gradually, Isabella was able to piece together a story. The professor was suffering from stomach cancer and could not move too far away. His plan was to stick to the large cities where there were specialists and plenty of medicine. Isabella caught up with the professor using methods that she refused to reveal. She explained that revealing her tactics would jeopardize her future investigations and make it more likely she would get her own throat cut.

The professor was convicted and sent to prison where he died shortly after being incarcerated. As for the victims of the swindle, the majority of their money was gone, but Isabella did recover enough for them to begin recovering rapidly and get back on the road to wealth. [34]

The case was satisfying to Isabella on a personal level, but it wasn't exceptional. In the wake of her fame and promotion due to the taxicab robbery case she continued doing what she did best – working the wide range of cases involving fortunetellers, fake doctors, and all manner of scammers trying to wrest away the money of innocent victims. She was still a woman in a man's world, but just about every policeman she encountered during her career spoke glowingly of Isabella and agreed that she deserved the promotion she had received.

Honest Dan Costigan was strongly inside the Isabella Goodwin fan club. When questioned by a reporter about the merits of women on the police force Honest Dan pointed out a recent arrest Isabella had made. The crook was a career criminal with intimate knowledge of the NYPD detectives and their methods. He had evaded arrest for several months until a frustrated Dan Costigan gave Isabella Goodwin a shot. Isabella left police headquarters at 10 o'clock in the morning with nothing more than a name and a photo. At noon she returned with her man.

The crook looked dejectedly at Costigan. "Yeah, she got me all right. I know all your bulls as far as I see em, but these women detectives have got me guessing. Why, it was as easy as pie for this woman. She came breezing along the street, piped me on the corner and then after lamping me good came over and asked where such and such hotel was. Of course, I fell for the gag and told her. She recognized the cut on my lip, flashed her badge, and the bull on the corner did the rest." The criminal shook his head. "It's sure tough on the crook these days. I've just finished a "bit" in Philly, which I'd never have done but for a swell looking girl detective, who had me spotted before I'd been in the town two hours. I tell you as long as a man is a man he'll trust a woman, so there's no use trying to make a getaway nowadays. There are bulls I know in the south who will tip me off every time I land in town, but if there's a woman detective in town – watch out. It won't be long before she'll buzzing around and get you right."

Isabella enjoyed busting the scam artists, especially as in the case of the grocery store owners when her arrest allowed the victims to avoid a complete financial catastrophe. It was fortunate that Isabella liked working these cases because there was no scarcity of the scammers in New York City during that era, especially fortunetellers. [35]

In 1993, almost seventy years after Isabella Goodwin turned in her detective shield to spend the remainder of her life in retirement, a restoration was underway at 97 Orchard Street in Lower Manhattan. Beneath the darkened floorboards of one apartment, left unchanged since the time Isabella trolled the streets on the lookout for scammers, a thin, frayed piece of paper from the 19th century was discovered; with one side printed in English and the other Yiddish, it advertised the fortune-telling specialties of "The World-Famous Palmist and Mind Reader", Professor Dora Meltzer.

Fortune-telling as a pastime and as a business can be found in a majority of cultures in the world. In New York's early immigrant communities, fortune-telling often came with a notion of exoticism, mixing mysticism with a foreign, sage-like edge. Many Jewish fortune tellers, like Dora Meltzer, used imagery that alluded to a Hebrew palm-reading manual dating to the 1500s called Khokhmes Hayad (The Wisdom of The Hand), or drew from the old-world appeal of Eastern Europe, where the practice was likely common in villages. [36]

In 1909 there were over one thousand fortune tellers plying their trade in New York City. Under names like psychic, prophet, and seer, they ran immensely profitable businesses that were supposed to have died out in the Middle Ages. No neighborhood was totally free from their influence. In the fashionable sections of the city the prophet or seeress had risen to the use of the telephone. It was in the poorer areas of the city where the scammers were found in surprisingly large numbers. It was estimated that in 1909 New Yorkers spent $10,000 daily on fortunetellers. The greatest portion of this sum was collected in very small amounts from those who could least afford to pay any money. In many of the neighborhoods populated by recent immigrants, prophets charged ten cents for their services. A great many of the scamming fortunetellers spoke the same language of the new arrivals, and with the superstitions believed by many in this population, these charlatans became powerful figures in their communities, similar to the stature of a clergyman or a family physician.

There was no service under the sun that these soothsayers would not perform. They were eloquent of their powers to restore missing relatives or friends. The longer a person was missing or the more valued the friendship, the higher the fee charged. Wives and husbands were located and diseases were cured. No field of usefulness was neglected. Especially when it came to the claims of medical cures, the police were eager to prosecute these scammers, but in a city the size of New York where so many languages were spoken, it was possible for quacks of the worst kind to work practically unmolested.

It may seem astonishing that these scammers could build a regular clientele who would return to them over and over again, but there were a number of simple tricks they used to gain a hold on their victims. One of the most familiar of these was to tell the name of a visitor, who was presumably, a complete stranger. To do this, an accessory stood by the door to take the visitor's hat and coat, and by a hasty examination secured the name or some scrap of personal information. Others made a point of telling whether the visitor was married or unmarried. In that case a mere guess would be right half the time. The amazing thing was that people would be so gullible. [37]

Isabella Goodwin never sought out any notoriety from the taxicab case. She just wanted to go on with her career being a detective. But when the spotlight was unavoidable, she handled herself with the upmost poise – most of the time. Even a professional like Isabella had a boiling point, which was reached when she was an invited guest to a luncheon during December of 1912.

Mrs. Alice Steuben Wells, wearing the light brown uniform and the silver badge of the Los Angeles Police Department was introduced as the first woman to serve on the uniformed force of any city in America. She was the guest of honor at the City Club's first Saturday luncheon of the season. She had not performed any recent policework because she had been on a leave of absence from her job for several months.

The large audience listened intently as Mrs. Wells described her job. Mrs. Wells sat on the right of toastmaster, Frederick H. Whitin, chairman of the City Club's committee on police. On his left, dressed very smartly sat Detective Isabella Goodwin. The City Club had asked her to speak, but in sending her to the luncheon Commissioner Waldo stipulated that she should not speak, explaining his stipulation by the time honored and phrase, "for the good of the service." In reality, Waldo believed publicity was no good for an effective detective.

When Mrs. Wells had taken her seat Mr. Whitin suggested that the prohibition should not be construed to prevent Mrs. Goodwin from asking any questions that occurred to her. Isabella waved off the host and said that Mrs. Wells had thoroughly answered any questions she might have had.

"You understand," Whitin said casually, "that Mrs. Goodwin is not a member of the uniformed force, but a detective."

"Ah," said Mrs. Wells, beaming down from the eminence of her little platform. "That's a shame. If you were in our city, you would be a regular police officer."

Mrs. Goodwin rose, her cheeks just a little pinker than usual. Perhaps she was embarrassed at being on her feet ready to defy her prohibition, but she didn't care. She had to speak. "I would have you understand," she said, "that I am a regular member of the police force." She then drew from a pocket a silver badge, the symbol of her rank of detective sergeant. "And what is more," she went on, "before I became a detective sergeant, I was a member of the uniformed force and did some work that you are supposed to be doing if you weren't on leave for so long." The tension in the room was palpable, but Mr. Whitin was quickly on his feet thanking everyone for attending such a lovely luncheon. [38]

...

During 1913 Deputy Commissioner Dougherty called on Isabella again to provide a crucial service. This time, however, her role had nothing to do with fortunetelling or a robbery investigation.

New York City is well known for its diverse and ethnic neighborhoods. One of these neighborhoods is Mulberry Street. Although it is the name of a street, it is also used to refer to the entire area. Little Italy originated in the 1880s, when immigrants from primarily, but not exclusively, Naples and Sicily arrived in New York City and settled in the streets between East Broadway and Houston and Centre/Lafayette Streets and the Bowery. Mulberry Street is a well-known as a principal thoroughfare, located in Manhattan in New York City. This area is historically associated with Italian American culture and history.

In order to get a better understanding of the area, The New York Times sent its reporters to characterize the Little Italy and Mulberry Street neighborhood back in May 1896. The writers noted that the residents there were all hard-working laborers; toilers in all grades of manual work; they were artisans, they were junkmen. It was noted that there was a "monster colony of Italians" who were considered to be the shop keeping community. The reporters found all sorts of stores, pensions, groceries, fruit emporiums, tailors, shoemakers, wine merchants, importers, and musical instrument makers. There were notaries, lawyers, doctors, and undertakers. But these hard-working immigrants looking to make their way in America is not the reputation Mulberry Street developed.

During the late 19th century, organized crime from Italy began to operate out of Mulberry Street. The Mafia families and gangs vied with each other for control of certain areas that included businesses. These business owners would have to pay a protection fee to the mob in order to have their shops untouched. Several well-known capos and families operated out of Mulberry Street. From the 1890's to the 1920's.

It was a mild spring evening on Mulberry Street on May 3, 1913. Sixteen-year-old Nellie DeCarlo lay in the bed of her second floor apartment at 241 Mulberry Street. Nellie knew all the local neighborhood gangsters, but she was too young and innocent to have any fear of them. Her most urgent concern on this evening was how to enjoy the cool night breeze flowing through her window while trying to tune out the street noises that accompanied the breeze. Nellie was accustomed to some noise from the street, but the voices from directly below her window were especially annoying.

Nellie arose from her bed and went to the window. The voices were coming from directly below her, so she leaned her head out the window and looked straight down to the sidewalk. A city streetlamp lit the sidewalk well, so Nellie had no trouble recognizing the people who were keeping her awake. It was her landlord, "Old man" Shillitano talking to his son, a 22-year-old she knew as the "Paper Box Kid." Nellie looked to the right and saw someone exit the pool room located at 235 Mulberry Street. As the man began walking north, she noted his derby and vest and recognized him as a neighborhood man named Frank Rizzo. Nellie then looked back down below her window and observed old man Shillitano pass a shiny object to his son. As Rizzo continued walking Nellie saw the Paper Box Kid, whose real name was Oreste Shillitano, approach Rizzo and raise his right arm. Nellie saw a bright flash and heard a loud bang that caused Rizzo to fall on the sidewalk. Nellie said the Young Shillitano turned and began to run north but was intercepted by a police officer who came running at him from the other side of Mulberry Street. She said that just as the officer was about to overtake Shillitano the officer raised his club and was about to strike, when Shillitano suddenly turned around and shot the officer. Nellie said she fell back onto her bed and did not look out the window again although several seconds after she returned to her bed she heard another shot, but did not return to the window.

Nellie DeCarlo didn't know it, but she had just been a witness to gang warfare. Besides being her landlord, Old Man Shillitano was a local gangster trying to exert control in the neighborhood that was being threatened by rival gangster, Frank Rizzo. Oreste Shillitano was going to step up as a neighborhood force to be reckoned with by eliminating Rizzo. The first part of the plan went well, as Rizzo never saw it coming when Shillitano stepped up to him and ended his ambition for more power, as well as his life. The plan quickly began to unravel, for Shillitano did not realize that just across the street Patrolman William Heaney was patrolling. As soon as the shot was fired, Heaney came dashing across the street in pursuit of Shillitano. Heaney was about to catch his prey, and he prepared to strike him with his club when Shillitano suddenly wheeled around and fired at point blank range at the officer. Heaney fell dead to the ground. Further north on Mulberry Street Patrolman Teare heard the two shots and ran to the scene. Shillitano never hesitated. When the cop approached, he raised his pistol and fired. Oreste Shillitano wanted to kill Frank Rizzo, but he had not planned on killing two New York City police officers. He also did not plan on a young girl at a second-floor window watching him commit the crimes. [39]

On May 5th Detective's Joseph Digilio and Leo Gambardella canvassed Mulberry Street, seeking information about the murders of Heaney, Teare, and Rizzo. Digilio smiled at the young girl standing outside the grocery store at 243 Mulberry Street before entering the store to speak to the proprietor. Gambardella remained on the sidewalk. He smiled at Nellie DeCarlo and attempted some casual conversation. "That was really something that happened around here the other night," the detective mentioned.

Nellie pointed up to the second floor of her building and said, "Oh yes, I saw it from my window.:

The detectives immediately whisked the girl away to police headquarters where she signed a statement reflecting that she had seen Oreste Shillitano shoot Frank Rizzo and Patrolman Heaney.

When Nellie went home and told her parents what had transpired at police headquarters her father became frantic when he learned his daughter had signed a statement reflecting that she had seen Shillitano commit the murders. Detective Digilio had been assigned to keep his eye on the building where Nellie lived, and when he learned that Nellie and her parents were extremely upset he brought the girl back to police headquarters.

Nellie told Deputy Commissioner Dougherty that her father told her she could be killed if she testified and that she would have to leave the house if she insisted on testifying. Dougherty didn't believe her and had Nellie's father brought to police headquarters where he confirmed that his daughter would not be welcome in his house if she intended to testify against Shillitano.

Dougherty sent Digilio with Nellie's parents to get some of her clothes and personal belonging, and then looked to a trusted source for help. He called Detective Sergeant Isabella Goodwin. For the next nine months Nellie DeCarlo lived with Goodwin and her 22-year-old daughter Margaret Goodwin at their residence of 136 Montague Street.

Nellie was frightened at first and woke up screaming in the middle of the first night at the Goodwin's home. Gradually, Nellie became comfortable and became very fond of Isabella. [40]

Nellie testified for the prosecution at Shillitano's trial but her father, Joseph DeCarlo, appeared for the defense in an attempt to negate his daughter's crucial testimony. Due in large part to Nellie's testimony, Oresto Shillitano was convicted and sentenced to die in the electric chair at Sing Sing.

Oresto's older brother, Johnny, who operated his father's poolroom on Mulberry Street, rounded up statements from four prosecution witnesses who recanted, including Nellie. The witnesses told their story to the world, and hearings were soon scheduled on whether to overturn the verdict. Nellie testified that Gambarbella and Digilio forced her to lie – that they put her in a room in police headquarters, lifted her chair to the ceiling and dropped it. "I came down all of a sudden and I fell unconscious," she claimed. "I fell unconscious for almost a few hours, and I had pains all over my body." She decided to come forward now, she said, because a priest at old St. Patrick's Cathedral had told her to do so in confession and refused to give her communion until she did.

Her story unraveled a bit when the prosecutor cross-examined her. Testimony from Isabella Goodwin helped save the conviction. Nellie had developed a close relationship with Isabella and her daughter during the nine months she lived with them. Isabella testified that Nellie had confided in her and her daughter that she had witnessed the murder.

The state's highest court upheld the conviction and Oresto Shillitano was executed on June 30, 1916 – but not before he fatally shot a prison guard in a brief escape a week before he was executed. [41]

With Nellie DeCarlo back with her family, Isabella got back to the familiar business of busting fortunetellers. Some of these scammers made her job ridiculously easy. At 338 West 22nd Street a sign announced that a demonstrator of immortality there pursues her mystic calling. Isabella went in and asked to see her dead sister, a sister who never existed. After a fee of fifty cents had been extracted, Isabella was led into a rear room shaded with black curtains. A white figure appeared in a minute or two murmuring, "Sister, my dear sister."

Isabella feigned emotion as she asked, "Are you happy?"

"Yes, I am very happy." That was all the spook would say as it glided away. Isabella's emotions vanished as she jumped for the thing in white and grabbed it by the wrist and dragged it to the window. Drawing the curtain, Isabella saw struggling in her grasp a pretty little blonde girl about seventeen years of age. Mrs. Goodwin had seen her on a previous visit to the house and recognized her as the daughter of the fortuneteller. [42]

The fortunetelling arrests were not always that easy, and sometimes things became physical. When Isabella focused her energies against the gypsy fortunetellers in Brownsville, Maria Marinda, alias "Jane the Gypsy," was arrested at 145 Christopher Street only after putting up a fight in which Mrs. Goodwin had to call out the reserves of the Brownsville station. Annie Luba of the same address was also arrested for trying to prevent the arrest. Isabella went to the house with

Detective George Christy and pointed out Marinda as the woman who she had obtained evidence against. Christy's attempt to arrest Marinda proved to be the signal for an attack from a dozen tenants in the house, with Luba trying to pull Marinda out of the grasp of the detectives. Christy had to use his billy club to protect Isabella. [43]

It wasn't only fortunetellers that Isabella targeted. Quack doctors were also fair game for the detective. Mrs. Emily Konice, known as Madam Elba, and Elizabeth Carter were charged with violating the health law and with being disorderly persons. Isabella Goodwin and Adele Priess, a matron whom Isabella would work regularly with, made the complaints. Isabella began the investigation on the complaint of a woman who paid Madame Elba $25 for treatment. When she went to the house the woman told madame Elba she was nervous and was prescribed a cure of olive oil soap and sweet oil. Miss Priess charged that Carter prescribed medicine for a supposed ailment and also told her fortune with cards. [44]

Isabella liked it best when an arrest ended up with a tangible positive result for the victim. When 47-year-old Elizabeth Herre, of Brooklyn was arraigned in court after being arrested by Isabella for fortunetelling, Daniel Gillesti was an interested spectator. Herre had broken up his family by getting his wife, Nellie, to turn over most of the furniture in their home in lieu of payment for telling her fortune. Gillesti said that as a result he and his wife had not spoken. Through Isabella's intervention Gillesti was able to recover his furniture but it was unclear if he was ever able to recover a good relationship with his wife. [45]

No detective is perfect. Even the best sleuths can get a case wrong. When Isabella Goodwin and Adele Priess entered 536 East 26th Street in Brooklyn, they thought they were simply dealing with another in a long line of quack doctors who were illegally practicing medicine. Isabella had visited Frederick Nowka on two occasions complaining of stomach problems, and on both occasions he massaged her abdominal area for an hour and charged her three dollars. Isabella's first indication that Nowka was no ordinary charlatan was at his hearing where the courtroom was filled with his supporters. [46]

Practically every member of the Central Branch of the YMCA had watched Nowka at work training men for various athletic events. Just about all the prominent bicycle riders several years earlier were under Mr. Nowka's care when he was in charge of the Manhattan Beach Bicycle Track. Nowka had been in charge of the physical training of many prominent people including at one time, Theodore Roosevelt. His supporters claimed that if Nowka was convicted of a crime, no athlete would be able to receive training. For his part, Nowka explained to the judge that he had merely performed a massage on Isabella, a technique he had utilized many times before on athletes. He went on to say that he was unaware that he needed a license to perform a massage. The judge quickly dismissed the charges. Isabelle and Adele Priess went back to work and Nowka went on to become a coach for the 1924 United States Olympic Team that competed in Paris. [47]

Along with her partner, Adele Priess, Mrs. Goodwin rounded up numerous men and women whom she charged with disorderly conduct, the charge that was used at the time to cover fortunetelling. After a while, however, the scammers began evolving to avoid Isabella's ever widening net. No longer were they advertising themselves as "specially gifted", with the ability to reveal the past, present, and future for a fee. Now, they were referring to themselves as "spiritualists," who depended on some kind of spiritual guide to reveal secrets. [48]

During February 1915, 53-year-old Margaret Hunt, of Brooklyn, the head of the Sunshine Spiritual Truth Society, was arrested for fortunetelling by Goodwin -but it wasn't Isabella. Isabella's daughter had followed in her mother's footsteps to a degree. Margaret Goodwin had not become a member of the police department, but as a private detective she had begun working with the police department on cases similar to the ones her mother was working. In this case, Margaret had attended a meeting in which Mrs. Hunt had invited the audience to ask questions of the medium. Ms. Goodwin arrested Hunt after she informed her that she had a brother in the European war. She had no brother. [49]

Just like her mother, Margaret would soon learn that not all of her arrests would be that simple. In the presence of a large number of spiritualists, who crowded the Gates Avenue court, Hannah Leo was examined by Magistrate Reynolds on the charge that she was a fortuneteller. The complaint against Miss Leo was made by Margaret Goodwin. Ms. Goodwin, who was not officially connected with the police department, declared that on the afternoon of January 26 she visited the spiritualist at the suggestion of Lieutenant Costigan, which came to her through her mother. She found a number of visitors assembled at a sort of séance presided over by Miss Leo. The spiritualist told her that the spirit of a girl slightly older than her had appeared and asked if Ms. Goodwin had forgotten her after she passed away several months earlier and was now surrounding Ms. Goodwin with flowers. Ms. Goodwin was also told that a man whose initial was "G" would ask her a question to which she must answer yes: that she would take a journey, have everything she wished for and would receive a gift.

At the hearing, Miss Leo was represented by Ralph Jacobs, who had frequently been counsel for various spiritualists in the courts. He asked Ms. Goodwin whether or not anything had been said about fortunetelling, and whether or not she had seen a charter from the Spiritualists Association of New York State and of the Society of the Golden Rule, hanging in Miss Leo's apartment. Ms. Goodwin stated that she had not, and also admitted that it was a meeting which she attended and not a private consultation. She also said she had not paid any money to Miss Leo but had given 25 cents to a man who took up a collection, adding he had told her to give the sum. Magistrate Reynolds decided that there had been no fortunetelling and granted Mr. Jacobs motion to dismiss the charge. [50]

As time went on Isabella found less fortunetellers to investigate. She did, however, find a marked increase in the number of "spiritualists" conducting business. These spiritualists, who had been fortunetellers at one time, now claimed to be heads of religious congregations, and claimed the protection under the law as set forth in a supreme court decision. [51] Isabella Goodwin had to battle the constitutional right to religious freedom to make some of her cases stick, but she never thought she would have to battle the authenticity of the practitioner.

After his arrest and subsequent conviction, W. Bert Reese was discharged by Judge Rosalsky in General Sessions on his appeal from a conviction by Magistrate Barlow of disorderly conduct, under the section dealing with fortune telling. Reese convinced Judge Rosalsky, Assistant District Attorneys Bostwick and Flint, and two reporters by demonstrations in court that he was not a disorderly person, but a man with apparently unusual powers."

Reese was arrested at 230 West 99th Street on February 26 on complaint by Detectives Isabella Goodwin and Adele Priess, who said they had paid him $5 to have their fortunes told. Reese denied that he had told their fortunes or accepted any money. He was found guilty and held in $1,000 bond to keep the peace for one year.

When his case came before Judge Rosalsky on appeal, Reese asked permission to demonstrate his abilities to the court. He told Judge Rosalsky to write something on each of three pieces of paper, and to fold them so that he might not be able to read what had been written. Judge Rosalsky put the papers in different pockets after he had mixed them up so that he could not distinguish them himself. Then Judge Rosalsky produced one of the folded papers and pressed it against Reese's forehead.

"You ask me how much money you have in a certain bank," Reese said. "Fifteen dollars is the answer."

Judge Rosalsky admitted that the answer was correct and produced the second piece of paper.

"This piece contains the name of one of your old schoolteachers Miss O'Connor," Reese said. The third question, which he read correctly but did not answer, was: What was the rule in Shelley's case?

Reese performed similar demonstrations for the benefit of Mr. Bostwick, Mr. Flint, and the reporters. His last feat was to give the maiden name of the mother of one of the reporters. All the questions were written on General Sessions stationery, which Judge Rosalsky supplied."

" 'I do not consider you a disorderly person," Judge Rosalsky said, when the demonstrations were finished. "You are honorably discharged." [52]

Despite some occasional setbacks, Isabella's work had become so well known in the fortunetelling community, threats were sometimes made by members of the occult profession. Such was the case during the testimony of Adele Priess. Ms. Priess identified the defendant in the courtroom as the person she had visited for a reading.

"The prisoner asked if I was Mrs. Goodwin, the detective," said Mrs. Priess, "and I told her I was not. 'If you are,' the defendant warned, 'I will place a curse on your life by my power.'" [53]

Isabella's work was not limited to scammers. Twenty-year-old John Hoffman lived with his well to do family on Fountain Avenue in Brooklyn. For several months Hoffman had become addicted to heroin and his parents had taken every means to rid their son of the habit, finally deciding to send him to a sanitarium. Before doing so, however, they decided an attempt should be made to find out from what source their son got his supply. The boy refused to reveal his source and the Brooklyn District Attorney said his investigation indicated that the source of the drugs was located in Manhattan, but he had no further information.

Isabella Goodwin and Adele Priess were put on the case to trail young Hoffman during his movements in New York City. After some days it was learned that he was a frequent customer at Benson's drug store, and finally, after much persuasion by Assistant District Attorney Wilmot, Hoffman agreed to aid the authorities in catching 48-year-old John Benson in the illegal sale of the drugs.

Hoffman had been instructed to telephone Benson that he would call in a half hour and the stage was set for capture. Soon Hoffman appeared, entered the store, walked toward the rear where Isabella was playing the role of a shopper. She observed Hoffman pass Benson $3 in marked bills in return for which the druggist handed Hoffman a bottle. Isabella provided a signal to Detective Deane, who entered the store and took the bottle from Hoffman and the marked money from the cash register. The bottle contained 300 heroin tablets, and Benson was immediately placed under arrest. [54]

Under the leadership of Honest Dan Costigan, NYPD Special Squad Number Two performed a range of undercover vice investigations, but between 1913 and 1918 their main investigative duty was policing abortion. Abortion was illegal in New York State between 1829 and 1970.

Policewomen had previously partnered with private medical interests to defend the boundaries of professionalism, with Isabella Goodwin working with a female detective of the New York County Medical Society to gain evidence against irregular practitioners. In this new squad Isabella Goodwin was teamed with Adele Priess. The two had worked together before and would become effective partners and good friends despite their different backgrounds. Goodwin was a working-class New Yorker, while Matron Adele Priess, who worked as a translator on investigations with Goodwin, was born in New York to parents from Alsace on the French-German border. She was a college graduate and learned German through having heard it spoken at home and worked as a language teacher before her marriage to a German migrant. [55]

Special Squad Two assembled a team of ambitious, experienced matrons, whose class and immigration status reflected the communities they sought to police. In a precedent-setting January 1913 case, Isabella Goodwin and Adele Priess visited a midwife's office at 333 East 79th Street, in the immigrant populated Yorkville neighborhood on Manhattan's Upper East Side. Matron Priess had a muddled conversation in German with midwife Pauline Papp, who would have preferred to use Hungarian. In their polyglot discussion, Priess explained that Goodwin missed menstruation, suffered morning sickness, and feared she was pregnant. They needed to end the pregnancy because she "was a widow, she works in an office, and her friend is a married man." Midwife Papp declined to give medicine and recommended instead that she undertake a pelvic examination, citing her twenty-three years of midwifery experience and training in Budapest. But Goodwin hesitated. Papp suggested that she go home instead, take a hot English mustard bath, wrap up warm, and return in the morning if these measures did not induce an abortion.

When the policewomen returned to Papp's office the next day, she agreed to perform an operation for twenty-five dollars. When the pair tried to haggle, she explained that while they may find someone that charged less, she knew how to do it "well and right." The women agreed and Goodwin lay on her back on the cold dining room table. She drew her knees up, placing her feet flat on the wooden surface, and lifted her skirts in preparation for the intimate exam. She felt the midwife's fingers inside her and saw her reach for surgical instruments. Papp positioned a syringe at the entrance to Detective Goodwin's vagina. At this moment, the policewoman announced she felt sick with nerves and her partner ran to the window, where she drew a handkerchief to her face. Two male officers waiting on the street recognized this gesture as a signal and entered the apartment. They arrested the midwife. [56]

Goodwin and Priess recounted these events on the witness stand in the court of General Sessions, where the case created new precedent: a woman did not have to be pregnant for the defendant to be guilty of an attempted abortion. Judge J. McLaughlin dissented and argued that Papp's case ought to be dismissed as "had the defendant succeeded in doing all that she intended to do she would not have committed the crime of abortion."

Although this complaint haunted the method, the NYPD deployed it as the primary means of policing abortion. The New York District attorney recorded twenty Special Squad Two cases against twenty-five defendants, but most investigations did not lead to indictments and Isabella Goodwin alone recalled working on forty such cases. [57]

The policewomen like Isabella were commended for their work in these abortion investigations, but they were also vulnerable to exploitation within the male world of policing. To reach the evidentiary bar of intent, plainclothes policewomen submitted to this intimate, invasive procedure in the line of duty. Not only did abortion investigations implicate their bodies, but lawyers and judges in the Court of General Sessions trials questioned policewomen's personal reputations; whether they were married, how many children they had, and their character. [58]

Chapter 5: The Women's Precinct

On January 29, 1918, Ellen O'Grady, a widow and former probation officer, became the first woman appointed to an executive level of the NYPD when she was named Fifth Deputy Police Commissioner. [59]

There were fifty-five men and eighteen women assigned to her office performing welfare work, but O'Grady also created a new "social welfare" squad under her direct supervision. In February 1918, she recruited Isabella Goodwin, Adele Priess, Maude Leslie, and Ada Brady for her squad. These four policewomen had previously comprised the abortion squad and would now also investigate complaints of assaults on women, wayward girls, fortunetelling, abduction, and domestic relations cases.

Isabella was greatly relieved when O'Grady denounced the method of investigating abortion cases and did away with the old custom that compelled a female representative of the Police Department to submit herself to a physical examination in order to gain evidence against abortionists. The manner of getting evidence was now less dangerous and not so degrading. O'Grady claimed that the old method was useless, with no convictions being possible because the female representing the police department was forced to voluntarily participate in the commission of a crime, and became, consequently, an accessory. She was astounded that nobody had seen the worthlessness of the practice before. [60] Goodwin got along well with Mrs. O'Grady, and she was put in charge of cases of juvenile delinquency, welfare work, vagrancy, and street fakers. [61]

Isabella also showed she could pursue her prey as well as the men. Fifty-year-old Frank Syron was panhandling in front of the St. George Hotel, and when confronting by Goodwin, he said he was getting a job in Manhattan and gave her the telephone number of the employer, telling her to call to verify his statement. As Goodwin walked over to a telephone booth, Syron fled. Goodwin gave chase and Syron was captured after going three blocks. He had been arrested nine times on similar charges and was sentenced to six months in jail for vagrancy. [62]

O'Grady's Welfare Bureau faced numerous organizational challenges. In 1919, she described her Women's Police Division as two forces, a paid force of eighteen and a volunteer corps of five thousand, known as the Women's Police Reserve. The reserve included wives and sisters of police officers as well as prominent social welfare workers trained under the supervision of regularly assigned members of the department. Although not officially members of the department, the Reservists wore uniforms and held infantry drills. Most of the reserve members were well-educated, upper-class women associated with progressivism and the various social betterment movements. The matrons were primarily working-class women, some of whom were widows who had entered the police department as a source of wages, rather than reformers.

O'Grady's appointment did not quell demands for adding more women, and on August 15, 1918, Police Commissioner Richard Enright named six women, including Mary Hamilton, to the uniformed force. In 1917, Mary E. Hamilton volunteered to assist the Missing Persons Bureau on cases involving young girls and women. Her offer was accepted and formed the basis for her later claim to be New York's first policewoman. The women were authorized to carry all the accoutrements that the policemen carried, including revolvers, handcuffs, and summons books, and had the same authority to question, detain, and arrest as male officers. However, the women did not wear uniforms and were viewed merely as an experiment. They were not considered members of the department and were exempt from civil service regulations which would permit their dismissal at any time.

Hamilton and O'Grady mirrored the differences between the Reserves and the matrons. O'Grady's social status was closer to the matrons than the reservists. A young widow with five daughters to support, she began a civil service career as a probation officer in the Brooklyn Magistrates Court in 1907. While working, she obtained a social work education and established ties with the Democratic Party. Her background, education, party loyalty, and the fact that she had worked with Mayor Hylan made her a perfect fit for the deputy commissioner post. Hamilton more readily fit the model of the reformist woman. She was not a career civil servant and seemed not to have worked until she volunteered her service for the police department. O'Grady was appointed because she was a friend of the mayor; Hamilton seemed to have been Commissioner Enright's choice. In fact, Hamilton and O'Grady clashed when Hamilton defied O'Grady's demands that women members of the department avoid getting involved in some of the political issues that were a constant feature of Enright's administration. Isabella was forced to take on a new, unenviable role, that of peacemaker as she tried to keep a lid on the growing hostility between O'Grady and Hamilton.

On January 3, 1920, Isabella Goodwin sensed something was wrong. Ellen O'Grady had called her into her office countless times before, and no matter what the situation was the Deputy Commissioner always had a friendly smile for her. On this day, however, Isabella was met with a somber frown. She quickly understood her boss's demeanor as she told a story to Isabella.

On the previous day a neighbor had visited Mrs. O'Grady at her Brooklyn home. The neighbor was the mother of a seventeen-year-old girl whom she had described as wild and hard to control at times, and during this visit the neighbor had her daughter with her. The mother and daughter proceeded to tell O'Grady about an incident that had happened to the daughter.

Two evenings earlier. The daughter and her seventeen year of friend were walking in Manhattan on Fifth Avenue near 56th Street. A big, beautiful limousine pulled to the curb next to them and a man got out of the car and began flirting with them. The man said he was an oil merchant and asked the girls if they would like to go for a drive through Central Park. Also in the car was a man who was identified as a railroad executive. While driving through the park, the oil merchant said he was having a "little party" at his Riverside Drive apartment and invited the girls to attend. When they got to the apartment the girls found that there was no party taking place and the daughter was sexually attacked by the oil merchant.

The mother said her daughter knew the man's name and the location of the apartment, and she immediately traveled to Riverside Drive to confront the man. The man tried to calm her and told her it was all a misunderstanding. Later in the day, the mother was contacted by a prominent New York law firm, and was told that if she was considering taking any action, she should do it in civil court so that they could settle the issue with a cash settlement. The mother rejected the offer and went to Mrs. O'Grady. [63]

Mrs. O'Grady obtained a warrant for the arrest of the oil merchant and assigned Isabella and Adele Priess, to arrest the man in his office. When Goodwin ad Priess arrived at the oil merchant's Wall Street office they were surprised to find two men present in the outer office, neither of whom were the oil merchant. Isabella was especially surprised at who these two men were. Greeting her with broad smiles were John C. Hackett, Police Commissioner Enright's personal secretary, and retired police inspector Edward Hughes, the owner of a detective agency and a close friend of Enright.

The two men did not actually prevent the women from entering the inner office to arrest the oil merchant, but they utilized all manner of meaningless small talk to delay their progress. Finally, when Isabella would be delayed no longer, she entered the inner office to find the room empty, noting a side door that provided another route out of the office. The two men simply shrugged and did not explain why they were in the office and denied knowing if the oil merchant had ever been in the inner office.

When Goodwin returned to headquarters and told Mrs. O'Grady what had transpired, the Deputy Commissioner was outraged. She feared that someone inside headquarters had leaked the information about the arrest warrant, which resulted in Hackett's presence in the office to attempt to prevent the arrest. Mrs. O'Grady already had a strained relationship with Commissioner Enright. She did not trust him, so she went directly to Mayor Hylan to explain what had happened. The mayor, in turn, notified District Attorney Edward Swann, who immediately initiated an investigation.

DA Swann called upon Enright to explain why his personal secretary and his good friend were at the office of a prominent oil merchant when Goodwin and Priess came to arrest him. O'Grady wanted to go public with the story, but Enright ordered her not to talk about the case.[64]

Retired Inspector Hughes made the statement that he had never been with Hackett in the oil merchant's office because he had been sick in bed for a week. This claim was ludicrous because both Goodwin and Priess knew Hughes and identified him as being in the office. Enright knew he had to do something to satisfy the District Attorney and to quell the rage of Mrs. O'Grady, so he accepted Hackett's resignation, claiming it was the culmination of complaints of questionable incidents, with this being the breaking point. In the meantime, an attorney for the oil merchant said he had traveled to Texas on business and would return in a week to surrender.

The investigation was all for nothing, as the grand jury refused to return an indictment. The girl and her friend testified along with a female physician and an unidentified male. The jurors decided there was not sufficient proof a crime had been committed. [65]

Isabella Goodwin continued her work in the Fifth Deputy Commissioner's Office, and Mrs. O'Grady's resentment of

Commissioner Enright continued to grow. A little after noon on December 13, 1920, Mrs. O'Grady burst into Commissioner Enright's office and flung her blue and gold shield on his desk and said, "I am leaving, Commissioner, I am through with the police department."

Without any discussion of her resignation, which she wished and understood to become effective immediately, Mrs. O'Grady walked out of the office she had held since January 29, 1918. O'Grady had been unhappy with the treatment she received from Enright from the beginning, especially almost a year earlier during the alleged sexual assault incident with the oil merchant. But she continued to put up with the indignities even though she felt she was being hampered in every manner of the performance of her job and that she was being treated like a dog.

Mrs. O'Grady reached the breaking point a few hours before she burst into Enright's office. Mary Hamilton had entered O'Grady's office and ignored her completely in directing Isabella Goodwin and several other members of O'Grady's staff to stop working on their current cases and to work with her on the Police Hospital Drive. [66]

The infighting between these women played a part in O'Grady's resignation, but prominent was her outsider status within the police department. She was far more concerned about vice and immorality than were rank and file members of the department, and although her background resembled that of many of the matrons and male police managers with whom she worked, her education and reformist agenda set her apart. She and Enright argued throughout her tenure. She resigned in a very public way, returning to her position as a probation officer.

She also alleged that Enright had interfered with inspections of movie theaters, a task frequently assigned to policewomen to ensure that films were not too suggestive and that advertising outside the theater met acceptable standards of decency

Word of the resignation spread quickly, and reporters quickly descended on Mrs. O'Grady's New York Avenue home in Brooklyn. When she met with the reporters her soft Irish voice was trembling with emotion, her blue eyes wide with scorn, indignities, and hurt pride. Flanked by her three daughters she spoke with frankness and fire. "I never knew before how men sell their souls and crawl for their bread and butter! But I'm a woman – and I won't crawl. No man should have the power to treat a woman as Commissioner Enright has treated me. No man should be permitted to crush a woman – or a man- who is doing right. Let the women of New York, the mothers, the members of women's clubs, ask why the morale of my department has been broken, why I have been humiliated at all times. I resigned when I found out I would no longer be allowed to give the women, the young girls, the children of New York a square deal as Deputy Commissioner in the police department!" [67]

"Since January 1919 I have been treated like a dog by Commissioner Enright. When I and my women detectives tried to arrest some men in his office for outrageous treatment to girls, you remember the case I refer to, ever since that time everything has been thrown in my way. It culminated this morning when Mrs. Mary Hamilton, a policewoman, came into my office and, ignoring me, told Acting Captain Ammon that she wanted two policewomen to help her work on the police hospital drive, naming Mrs. Sullivan, Mrs. McCarthy, and Mrs. Goodwin. She said that all three women were to work on the hospital drive. Mrs. Hamilton wanted to use these three women for the police hospital drive, and when I wanted women to search for missing girls, I could not get them. A man came into my office this morning and said he had reported his sister missing to the Missing persons Bureau. They promised to send a woman detective on the case, and he begged me this morning to send a woman detective, as no attention had been paid to his complaint. There seems to be no women available in the Missing Persons Bureau now, for they are all working on the hospital drive. Last month, a mother abandoned her four children. I wanted a woman detective to work on the case, but I could not get one, and I had to work on it myself. They have taken my car away from me, and when I asked for one, Enright said, 'You can't have a car.' All this happened after I started to investigate the workings of a man in his office. I was sick recently and four days' pay was taken out of my salary. I asked Mayor Hylan for a car, and he refused to let me have one. When my detectives went to enforce the law in a number of moving picture houses, the managers of these houses showed them receipts stating that they had contributed to the police hospital fund and they had been promised that no police action would be taken against them. When I used strenuous efforts to enforce the law in the dancehalls of this city, that work was taken away from me. [68]

When Mrs. O'Grady tossed her badge on Enright's glass top desk and cried, "I'm through!" the commissioner did not consider the act an official resignation without a written document. That administrative problem was solved when O'Grady's daughter, Florence, who acted as her mother's personal secretary, traveled to police headquarters carrying a large, important-looking envelope which contained Mrs. O'Grady's official letter of resignation. Also included in the envelope was the resignation of Florence herself as secretary to the Fifth Deputy Commissioner. [69]

Once Enright was satisfied that the resignation was official, he had the following entry made into official police department records.

Whereas, on the 13th day of December, 1920, at about 12:30 o'clock in the afternoon of the said day, Fifth Deputy Police Commissioner Ellen A. O'Grady entered the office of the police commissioner in a hysterical condition, and in a loud, boisterous, insolent, and insubordinate manner threw the shield of her said office upon the desk of the Police commissioner and at the same time exclaiming, "I am through with the police department," and having immediately thereafter abandoned the said office and refused to perform the duties duly assigned to said office in accordance with law.

Ordered, that her said resignation is hereby accepted effective forthwith.

Whereas Florence E. O'Grady, stenographer to the Fifth Deputy Police Commissioner, having on or about 12:30 P.M. Dec. 13, 1920, abandoned her said position in this department and has absented herself without leave, now therefore it is:

Ordered, That the said stenographer be and she is hereby dismissed from the service of the Police Department of the City of New York effective forthwith. [70]

With his official duty regarding the resignation completed, Enright took a swipe at O'Grady's social class. Enright, who was the first commissioner to have risen from within the ranks, declared that her principal grievance was that she was not furnished with an attractive, high-prices limousine automobile to enable her to conduct her social and shopping business in the style which she considered as befitting her high office. There was nothing in O'Grady's background to indicate she was accustomed to limousines, but she and Enright had battled over her department car, which she believed should have been replaced. He also claimed she was annoyed at not having been permitted to attend conventions in different parts of the country at the expense of the city, and that she was aggravated by having to complete a lot of paperwork when her handbag, containing her police credential was lost.

When O'Grady resigned it was strongly rumored that Isabella Goodwin would be appointed as Fifth Deputy Commissioner. Her experience and record, which displayed an ability to avoid problems and controversy, combined with the mayor's penchant for appointing deputy commissioners from within the uniformed ranks seemed to make Isabella the ideal candidate to succeed Mrs. O'Grady. It was never clear whether Isabella really sought the deputy commissioner position. Some said she would have welcomed the position, but others pointed to the fact that in accepting a civilian position she would had had to give up her pension rights – something they said she would never do. The mayor had about 200 applications for the job from women who were prominent in all sorts of civic, ethical, and sociological organizations. [71]

While waiting for O'Grady's replacement to be named, something big in the world of women's policing in New York City was brewing. For the first time in history New York City would have a police precinct run exclusively by and for women. In a move that Isabella never really conveyed her feelings about, Mary Hamilton was appointed to direct the new precinct while Isabella Goodwin was assigned as officer in charge. [72]

The Women's Precinct became a reality in March 1921. The concept of the precinct was influenced by the defined women's role of the era, which primarily involved the home, children, and care for the less fortunate. This led to the belief that women should help other women and support their natural maternal roles. They saw themselves as protectively assuming moral guardianship over women and children coming into contact with the police.

New York's progressive era reformers had aided in expanding the role of women in the police department beyond the simple matron duties – a movement that had greatly benefitted Isabella Goodwin. New York City, however, was not eager to join the movement. Only the coming of World War I, which brought renewed concerns about prostitution, sexual immorality, and venereal disease, led the city to act. Comprised primarily of social workers and civic leaders, the women's committee of the Mayor's Committee on National Defense urged Police Commissioner Arthur Woods to use the war emergency powers granted him in August 1917. He responded by appointing two women special patrolmen, authorizing them to make arrests but exempting them from civil service.

There were many controversies over appointment of policewomen in a number of cities, but the size and political complexity of the New York City Police Department added to the difficulties. One of the groups most vigorously opposed to Commissioner Enright's appointment of the six policewomen were women. The existing police matrons received a lower salary than the new policewomen, and the matron believed that the new women, with a higher social status and educational attainment, would replace them in the few non-custodial tasks they had managed to carve out for themselves.

Despite the disputes between O'Grady and Enright and the split between the Reserve women and the career women in the police department, the Women's Precinct opened in March 1921, only four months after O'Grady's resignation, with Mary Hamilton as its director. Isabella Goodwin, along with twenty patrolwomen and six policewomen were assigned to the precinct, officially designated the Special Duty Division. The precinct, which Hamilton said was her idea, included detention areas, a clinic and temporary hospital for the care and venereal disease testing of the girls in custody, and classrooms in which policewomen would receive their training.

Among the speakers at the precinct's official dedication on May 3, 1921, were Mayor Hylan, Commissioner Enright, city commissioners and police officials. Social service workers and wives of city officials also attended. Noting that the precinct, in what had been a rundown station house on 37th Street between Ninth and Tenth Avenues in Hell's Kitchen, "had been transformed by feminine hands," The New York Times observed that, "All the windows in the station are now screened with white curtains and... on the window ledges are boxes containing flowers...In the office of Mrs. Hamilton hangs a canary in a wicker cage, which yesterday was singing gaily."

It was decided that one of the most important functions to be carried out at the Women's Precinct was the solution of the problem of the detention of girls and women who had committed no crime, and were not immoral, nor delinquent, but who, for some reason or other, had to be temporarily detained. [73]

Several lieutenants were temporarily assigned to the Women's Precinct, for the purpose of instructing patrolwomen in the proper method of making official records, as well as handling the different conditions that may come within the scope of that department. Twenty-five of the police and patrolwomen assigned to the Women's Precinct received diplomas at the exercises held there. The course consisted of about five weeks work in first aid to the injured, and police practice, under the auspices of the Training School at Police Headquarters. The diplomas issued to the women were furnished by the Society for Instruction in First Aid to the Injured.

The basement contained baths, and a room where clothing could be fumigated. Should a woman defendant be ill, or appear not in good health, she would be given medical attention, and if necessary, a nurse. Part of the second floor was fitted up as a hospital.

The second floor also contained the "sleeping apartments," which were quite different from the usual police station cells. They had been so arranged that a woman, hardened by misfortunes, would not be thrown with the girl or woman who had run afoul of the law for the first time, to the detriment of the latter. While the girl was staying in the Women's Precinct, she would have the opportunity to do a little work. A workroom and equipment were provided. There was a hostess committee which would arrange to show the runaway girls something of New York before they were returned to their parents or guardians. The only negative tone regarding the precinct was sounded by the chief magistrate, who questioned the legality of using the facility as a place of detention.

By the time of the precinct's official opening, it was already rife with internal dissention. When O'Grady resigned, Isabella Goodwin had been appointed acting deputy commissioner, but when the precinct opened Hamilton was named director, with Goodwin her deputy. The dissension only got worse a month later when Isabella found herself passed over again. The Fifth Deputy Police Commissioner title was not filled. But the command structure was further confused when on May 12, 1921, Mrs. Julia Loft was named an Honorary Deputy Police Commissioner in charge of welfare work to succeed O'Grady. Loft was also put in charge of the Women's Precinct, and Hamilton now reported to her. A number of prominent citizens were designated honorary deputy commissioners at that time. The title indicated that they did not come from the ranks and had never been sworn as police officers. The designation had nothing to do with Mrs. Loft's assignment or her sex. Loft immediately announced that, despite her honorary designation, she planned to be at her desk every day and would occasionally work nights. Hamilton was now Loft's assistant in charge of the women police.

Loft was unlike O'Grady or Hamilton. She was neither a career civil servant nor a trained social worker. Her husband, a one-term Democratic Congressman from New York City who supported Tammany Hall, was a wealthy candy manufacturer whose horses raced at Saratoga and who owned homes in Baldwin, Long Island, and in Palm Beach, Florida. Although now the wife of a prominent, wealthy man, Julia McMahon Loft was one of five children of a New York City Police Officer. She met her husband, a widower, when she worked as a saleswoman in his Barclay Street store, and they were married on June 17, 1911.

Mrs. Hamilton, who had no idea that another woman would be put over her, established herself in the best office in the building, a cozy snuggery right at the entrance on the main floor. She moved in all her office equipment, including her pet canary, Mickey.

A case could be made that Mrs. Loft was responsible for the death of the bird, although the new honorary deputy commissioner was innocent of murderous motive. On the day of Mrs., Loft's installation she was photographed with Commissioner Enright eight times by flashlight in Mrs. Hamilton's office. The explosive powder was too much for Mickey. When the great day of jubilation was over, Mickey lay dead in his cage. Mrs. Hamilton was in tears over his still form, and Mrs. Loft had her eye on Mrs. Hamilton's office, which she felt was the appropriate quarters for the top woman at the precinct.

Everyone tried to put their best face on as Enright stood between the two ladies while the police band played "Dear Old Pal." As Loft's appointed assistant, Isabella Goodwin also stood uncomfortably by as the band played.

Five weeks later Isabella had assumed her familiar role of peacemaker, this time trying to quell the open hostility between Mrs. Loft and Mrs. Hamilton. Hamilton had not taken the hint regarding the office, and Mrs. Loft had been compelled to take a smaller, less desirable office three flights up. The stairs were steep and Mrs. loft considered it undignified for herself and her many visitors to mount them. Finally, Mrs. Loft demanded that Mrs. Hamilton give her office. [74] She also designated Isabella Goodwin as her chief assistant. [75]

In assuming her position Mrs. Loft made a speech of only two sentences. She said she could not talk about her work until she had done it, and she promised to do all she could for the boys and girls of New York City and elsewhere. [76]

Goodwin celebrated her 25th anniversary and spoke about the Women's Precinct. "I thought I knew a lot about police methods, but this new police precinct is teaching me new things every day. I believe if we save just one boy or one girl every six months our precinct will be worth all the time and effort that has been given to its establishment. But already our records show real results." [77]

Whether at her own or the mayor's initiative, Loft was quick to bring changes to the Women's Precinct. On June 25th, after clashing with Loft over the lodging facilities the chief magistrate had questioned, Hamilton was removed from the precinct and transferred to police headquarters.

Hamilton was a divisive figure within the department. Her repeated claims to be New York's first policewoman, even though matrons had been hired many years earlier, did not endear her to the women of the department. Isabella Goodwin, whom Hamilton eclipsed at the Women's Precinct, was more popular with colleagues and had garnered excellent publicity for women officers including urging that the role of matrons be expanded. Hamilton's outspokenness and her high visibility were most likely what led Mayor Hylan to have favored the appointment of first O'Grady and then Loft to curtail these qualities. Although the Special Duty Division continued to operate from the precinct, it attracted less attention and was dissolved in September 1923.

Mrs. Loft had already resigned during January 1923. Besides her conflicts with Mary Hamilton, Loft's tenure was best remembered by her campaign to keep "women of questionable character" out of the city's dance halls. She also objected to such dances as the Chicago, the Toddle, the Camel Walk, and the Collegiate, the popular jazz steps of the day. [78]

Slightly two years after its heralded opening, the precinct's welfare functions were absorbed into a unit that in March 1924, Enright placed under Hamilton's supervision. In November, the unit which contained about 100 women officers and operated out of police headquarters, was designated the Women's Bureau, and the women assumed such traditional police functions as patrolling dance halls, movie theaters, recreational piers, parks, railway terminals, subways, elevated train stations, and ferries. They also participated in crime prevention and social welfare functions. They did not maintain any detention or lodging facilities anywhere in the city. By 1926, the precinct was forgotten. It was not even mentioned in a full-column story on Hamilton's resignation from the police department on January 26, 1926. [79]

Chapter 6: The End of a Career

When Isabella's oldest daughter, Marjorie, was grown and out of the house, Isabella moved from Perry Street to a rooming house on Hoyt Street in Brooklyn. Among the other residents were several young men, including one Oscar Seaholm. He earned a steady living as an advertising solicitor for a newspaper. He had been born in Connecticut, had served honorably in Meuse-Angonne for the American Expeditionary Forces during World War I, and had a brother who was the key designer for Cadillac. But, more significantly, Oscar Seaholm had spent his lifetime studying with some of the greatest music teachers in the country and was a frequent baritone soloist in New York's largest churches. Later, he would even tour the West Coast and appear in movie shorts for Paramount Pictures, so handsome was he. Isabella Goodwin could tune in to WRNY to hear him sing opera. He was twenty-three years old in 1920. By many accounts, she was a young-looking fifty-five. Neither of them was married. But, by November of 1921, they would be. [80]

Isabella did not announce her marriage and it wasn't until two weeks after she was wed that anyone on the department or in the press learned of her nuptials. Even when her marital status was discovered Isabella remained tight lipped about her private life. "Why should anyone care if I am married or not?" she asked. "I consider it a personal matter and don't intend to say anything about it," she declared. [81]

On December 2, 1924, Isabella decided 28-years was enough and filed for retirement from the New York City Police Department. After she announced her retirement, she sat to answer the questions of reporters.

"Last summer, I bought a little place in Maine, near Gardiner," she said. "My friends want me to start a detective agency. And of course, there is big money to be made in private work. But for a while, anyhow,

I'm retiring. My family wants me to spend more time with them, and I'm crazy about antiques."

"What do you consider your most exciting case," asked a newspaperman.

"That of the Church Street Bandits," Isabella answered. "Because for nine days and nights I lived with them, in constant watch of my life. If I had made one false move a knife would have been plunged into me. But there is always danger of every kind in detective work – and sometimes the danger is greater when you do not appreciate it and are not on your guard."

"What are the qualifications for a woman detective?" a reporter asked.

"The first is discipline," Isabella stated. "Women are less amenable to this than men. Then she must be shrewd and quick at expedients. Fully as valuable to her will be the quality of intuition, to sense things for which at first, she has no actual proof. Perhaps it is because of greater intuition that women sometimes succeed when men fail. They have more intuition, if less discipline." Isabella continued, "Then, the woman detective must be a good mixer. She must be able to make acquaintances among all classes. She must, in addition, have self-control and courage. Finally, she must have the hound's trick of never giving up the trail once she starts on it."

Isabella spent the last year of her career working for Joab H. Banton, the District Attorney of New York County, doing what she did when she started her detective work – arresting scammers. [82]

Isabella was a great person and was truly inspirational. She died of colon cancer at the age of 78 on October 26th, 1943 and is buried in the beautiful Green-Wood Cemetery in Brooklyn as Isabella Seaholm. She may have been New York's first female detective and there on the job long before the NYPD hired its first official female cop, but I'm sure she would be proud of the fact that, today, the NYPD has 6,724 female officers. Among them are chiefs, inspectors, captains, lieutenants, sergeants, and detectives, just like Isabella was. She firmly believed that women make better detectives than men.

The first female detective in New York City, Isabella started her police career as a matron, scrubbing the jail cells and acting as a glorified babysitter for the pleasure of $6 a week, but using her incredible undercover capabilities, she cracked one of the hardest cases the NYPD had ever faced leading to her promotion to detective and a salary of nearly $3,000 a year, only around $8,000 less than what a long-term officer in New York today earns in today's money. Many other great female detectives followed Isabella, but as a poor single mother of four living in the roughest part of a New York consumed by violence and poverty, to rise to a position of power that was the detective lieutenant shield, it is a story of her courage, her intelligence and her phenomenal sleuthing skills. Isabella Goodwin was extraordinary. And nothing less.

Women make strong detectives because of their ability to sense things for which at first you have no actual proof. I think that the reason why a woman sometimes succeeds where a man fails is because she is more strongly endowed with this intuition. I was proud to show just what a woman can do when the chance comes her way."– Isabella Goodwin.

IMAGE GALLERY

Isabella Goodwin and a detective outside police headquarters

Isabella Goodwin

Bibliography

1. Keynote Remarks at the 2015 Women in Policing Conference: "Women in the NYPD: Hear Them Roar" Mary Jo White New York, New York Oct. 20, 2015
2. The Day Book, December 28, 1912, page 5 and 6
3. NYS SURPREME COURT, 1893
4. The Sun, January 06, 1890, p1
5. The Sun, 1/10/1895, p7
6. The Fearless Mrs. Goodwin, Elizabeth Mitchell, Byliner Inc., 2011
7. The Sun, 7/10/1895, p2
8. The Fearless Mrs. Goodwin, Elizabeth Mitchell, Byliner Inc., 2011
9. The Sun, 12/31895, p8
10. The Fearless Mrs. Goodwin, Elizabeth Mitchell, Byliner Inc., 2011
11. Seagrave, Kerry, Policewomen: A History, 2d ed. - Page 13
12. The Fearless Mrs. Goodwin, Elizabeth Mitchell, Byliner Inc., 2011
13. The Fearless Mrs. Goodwin, Elizabeth Mitchell, Byliner Inc., 2011
14. The Sun, Nov. 1, 1891, p25
15. Jackson, Women Police, 110–3
16. Seagrave, Kerry, Policewomen: A History, 2d ed. - Page 13
17. Collins, James H, The Great Taxicab Robbery, A True Detective Story, 2016
18. Collins, James H, The Great Taxicab Robbery, A True Detective Story, 2016
19. New York Times, Answers to questions about New York, Michael Pollak, Jan. 18, 2013
20. The Sun, February 16, 1912, p 1 and 2
21. New York Tribune, 2/16/1912, p1 and 2

22. Collins, James H, The Great Taxicab Robbery, A True Detective Story, 2016

23. The Evening World, 2/29/1912, p16

24. The Sun, February 27, 1912, Page 3

25. The Day Book, 2/27/1912, p29

26. Whalen, Bernard, Undisclosed Files of the Police, 2016

27. The Evening World, 2/28/1912, p2

28. Mullenbach, Cheryl, Women in Blue, Chicago Review Press Inc, 2016

29. The Sun, 2/27/1912, p3

30. The Sun, 2/27/1912, p1

31. The Evening World, 3/1/1912, p1

32. Mullenbach, Cheryl, Women in Blue, Chicago Review Press Inc, 2016

33. The Sun, 3/2/1912, p16

34. Ottumwa tri-weekly Courier, July 22, 1916, p3

35. The Brooklyn Daily Eagle 11/28/15, p27

36. Zarrelli, Natalie, The Hidden World of Tenement Fortune Tellers in 19th Century Manhattan, December 4, 2015

37. New York Times, 12/12/1909, p55

38. New York Times, 12/15/1912, P15

39. Forgotten New York, Mulberry Street, Little Italy, 12/16/018

40. NYS Court of Appeals Records and Briefs, 1916

41. Moses, Paul, The Italian Squad, 2023

42. New York Times, 5/11/1913, p3

43. The Brooklyn Daily Eagle, 2/12/14, p16

44. The Brooklyn Daily Eagle, 2/22/14, p22

45. The Brooklyn Daily Eagle, 5/10/14, p32

46. The Brooklyn Citizen, 7/9/14, p12

47. The Brooklyn Citizen, 10/16/13, p5

48. The Brooklyn Daily Eagle, 3/10/14, p12

49. The Standard Union, 2/13/15, p2

50. The Brooklyn Daily Eagle, 3/18/15, p2

51. The Brooklyn Daily Eagle, 1/24/15, p8

52. Future and Cosmos, when a case was won by mindreading, Monday, December 27, 2021

53. The Standard Union, 12/10/12, p1

54. The Brooklyn Daily Eagle, 6/30/14, p18

55. People v. Pauline Papp, Jan. 10, 1919, p. 7, trial 1760, reel 318, New York Court of General Sessions,

56. People v. Papp, 7.

57. People v. Bertha Schmulenson, Jan. 10, 1919, p. 16, case 2551, reel 318, NYCGS.

58. NYC DEPARTMENT OF RECORDS & INFORMATION SERVICES

59. The Brooklyn Daily Eagle, 2/12/1918, p3

60. NYPD, "Annual Report" (New York, 1918), 89.

61. The Brooklyn Daily Eagle, 2/14/1918, p14

62. The Brooklyn Citizen, 8/6/1920, p2

63. The New York Herald, 1/6/1920, p4

64. The New York Herald, 1/4/1920, p20

65. The New York Herald, 1/8/1920, p3

66. The Evening World, 12/13/1920, p1

67. The Evening World, 12/15/1920, p26

68. The Brooklyn Daily Eagle, 12/13/20, p1

69. The New York Tribune, 12/16/1920, p3

70. The Evening World, 12/24/1920, p2

71. The Brooklyn Daily Eagle, 2/7/1921, p16

72. The Standard Union, 5/2/21, p7

73. 1921 NYPD Annual Report

74. The Brooklyn Daily Eagle, 12/31/1922, p17

75. Times Union, 5/13/1921, p11

76. The Brooklyn Daily Eagle, 5/17/1921, p3

77. Times Union, 5/17/21, p6
78. The New York Times, 5/17/62, p37
79. Moss, Dorothy, A Precinct of their Own, 2004 p39-55
80. The Fearless Mrs. Goodwin, Elizabeth Mitchell, Byliner Inc., 2011
81. The Standard Union, 11/28/21, p13
82. The Brooklyn Daily Eagle, 11/2/24, p16